Rainy Day Miracle

A Remarkable Story of Healing and Faith

Jill & Matt Cheatham

Rainy Day Miracle: A Remarkable Story of Survival and Healing
Published by Open Field Media
Broadlands, IL

ISBN: 979-8-218-66214-1

BIOGRAPHY & AUTOBIOGRAPHY / Memoirs

Cover and interior design by Asya Blue, copyright owned by Matt and Jill Cheatham

This story is entirely true. Some names have been changed to protect identity.

QUANTITY PURCHASES: Schools, companies, professional groups, clubs, and other organizations may qualify for special terms when ordering quantities of this title. For information, email rainydaymiracle@gmail.com.

Printed in the United States of America.

OPEN FIELD
MEDIA

To the first responders, emergency room personnel, surgeons, doctors and nurses that worked to save and heal me.

CONTENTS

PROLOGUE

Early Monday morning on October 11, 2021, Matt Cheatham, an employee with a pipeline maintenance company, headed to work. His work crew had recently moved material and equipment to a remote job location near the Wabash River in Terre Haute, Indiana. Maintaining pipes for oil companies was a grueling job, and he was accustomed to working in hot or cold, wet and dirty conditions to make sure pipe remains underground and functioning properly.

That particular day, the weather was sunny and pleasant. But weather is temperamental and, over the day, the sky darkened, the wind sweeping dirt into little dervishes across the work site. A storm was moving in. The crew kept an eye on the radar to see how close the front was moving and how much longer they could keep working. Eventually, it began to rain, so the crew packed up and headed south to return to the shop.

Instead of going back with the crew, Matt headed west toward home. The wind buffeted his vehicle, picking up the farther west he drove. Tree branches swayed on either side of the road while fallen leaves skittered across the pavement. Rain pelted Matt's windshield though the steady *thump, thump, thump* of the windshield wipers did little to improve visibility.

Without warning, there was a loud creaking—a deafening crash—and Matt was jolted into the ditch. When he was able to get his bearings, he noticed that his window was shattered. His gaze travelled to the driver's side windshield which was punctured through with a tree branch.

He followed the tree branch from the window down to his chest. *Through* his chest.

Death seemed to open the door in that moment, whispering, "Come with me, Matt."

He tried to wrap his brain around what just happened. *I need help.* Before the pain set in, before he lost consciousness completely, he whispered, "watch over me and protect me."

"So do not fear, for I am with you;
do not be dismayed, for I am your God.
I will strengthen you and help you;
I will uphold you with my righteous right hand."

(Isa 41:10) New International Version

DAY OF THE ACCIDENT

MORNING

By 5:15 a.m. every morning, I was already in the kitchen, my robe wrapped tightly around me and the smell of fresh-brewed coffee wafting through the room. Matt left for work by 6:00 a.m. every day, and it had become a normal part of our routine that I had his lunch packed as he fixed our thermoses.

I worked as an elementary school teacher and noticed that the day was dreary, the sky filled with low-hanging, dark clouds. It would be an indoor recess day.

Matt slid my coffee cup across the counter. I caught it with the deft practice of those familiar morning routines. My mind wandered as I sealed Tupperware containers and made sure his water bottle was full.

"Let me know if you hear anything," he called as he headed toward the bathroom to get in the shower.

"You bet," I answered as his steps faded down the hallway. We were expecting word any day of the birth of our very first great-nephew. I checked my phone once more, excited for any news. It would be the first time there would be a baby in the family in a long time.

Matt and I had just celebrated our 25th wedding anniversary on June 29, 2021. Our life together was full of many blessings but, like most everyone, we'd also navigated some trying times.

When we were in our mid 20's, we met in 1995 at the Martinsville Agricultural Fair. Apparently, while I had been complaining to my cousin about not being able to find anyone I liked or wanted to date, Matt, who was a friend of hers too, had been doing the same when they hung out. So, mischievous friend that she was, she arranged a meeting at a snow cone stand. Little did I know that Matt's mother owned the snow cone stand and that Matt was going to be there, too.

The heat was oppressive that day and sweat dripped down the back of my neck, creating damp trails on the back of my shirt. The snow cone was refreshing, and Matt was pleasant, full of smiles and easy conversation. When I didn't know what else to say, I shrugged and went to ride the amusement rides with a younger girl from my church.

Matt was waiting for me when I got off the ride. He asked for my number that day and called within a week to ask me on a date. God had put us together and we didn't need a lot of time to know that we were a match made in heaven. We had both grown up on farms and in Christian homes. Within a year, during summer vacation from teaching, we were married.

As in any marriage, our relationship had its share of fluctuations. At the time of our marriage, I had been teaching for four years. During my fifth year, I had a student teacher who talked about the teaching positions available in California. I interviewed and got a job and we moved to California as newlyweds. We joined a church there and became a part of a small group for young couples without kids. Only two years later, we moved back home to be closer to family and so Matt could get his degree in aviation. I didn't start back in the classroom right away, but instead took a job at a family-owned business in the office entering data into the sales system.

In May of 2001, at the end of Matt's degree, we had our first child. Nicole was a wonderful blessing. The summer Matt graduated, I stepped back into the classroom, and we moved again. I remember my mother teasing me about how many mailing addresses we had.

We settled in Champaign, Illinois, Matt got a job, and I started teaching again. Two years later, in 2003, our son Ryan was born. Up until that point in my life, I hadn't ever experienced what I would call trauma, but Ryan's birth certainly was. Born by C-section, my sweet boy initially had trouble breathing. He needed to stay in the NICU for ten days, some of which time he spent fully intubated. My own recovery was painful, but nothing could have prepared Matt and I to see our tiny son with all manner of tubes attached to him, like some awful science experiment. Nearly two weeks later, Ryan was finally healthy enough to go home. While he has no memory of what he went through, the events of those days stayed with my husband and I so clearly. I learned then that when situations occur that aim to rip your heart from your chest, it forces you to really lean on God, to stop and think and find trust in Him again. We made it through, and we were blessed.

Blessed for sure, I thought as Matt's voice returned me to the present.

"Is the lunch ready?"

"Mmhmm," I said, handing him his insulated lunch container. He kissed me on the cheek, snagged his water bottle from the refrigerator, and headed out the front door. In under half an hour, I, too, was out the door and headed to school.

Matt sent me his silly texts throughout the day, asked about who was going to be home first to take care of the pets, and whether I wanted chicken casserole for dinner. When he asked me if I had any meetings after work (I almost always did), I surprised him by saying there weren't any on schedule just a quick errand and then I'd be home.

By the time the school day ended, I was exhausted, so I spent only a little time putting my classroom back in order and checking in with a colleague. As I gathered my things, I noticed a missed call from Matt on my phone.

Sorry I missed your call, I texted back. *Leaving work now. See you at home soon!*

When I got home, I began fixing chicken and noodles for dinner, with extra servings so Matt and I could take some to our daughter and her husband later that evening. By the time the oven timer sounded, I noticed it was already 5:10 P.M. Matt should have been home already.

I grabbed my phone and sent him a quick message: *When will you be home?*

Less than a minute after I hit send, the phone rang. Matt's name popped up on the caller ID, but when I answered it was definitely not Matt's voice on the other end.

"Hello?" a woman's voice answered.

"Who is this?" I asked, gripping the phone tightly.

"My name is Bonnie and I'm a nurse at the hospital," the woman said. "Are you related to Matthew Cheatham?"

"Yes." Anxiety pooled in my gut, acrid and nauseating. Something was wrong.

"Your husband was brought into the ER this evening. He was involved in an accident and is currently being taken to surgery..."

Bonnie's voice dimmed in my mind as my body immediately lurched into action. Fog filled my head, filtered through with only the essentials.

A bag with a few haphazardly thrown items of clothing. A toothbrush. A hairbrush. Cellphone charger. Far away, I heard Bonnie's voice as she filled in the details of Matt's accident. Matt was in Indiana, and I was about an hour and a half away.

He had been impaled by a tree limb that had shattered the front windshield of his car, puncturing straight through the middle sternum portion of his chest.

No wonder he hadn't texted me back.

Why did I wait so long to text to see when he would be home?

How could this be happening?

So many more ideas, thoughts, and wonderings ran through my head. I explained to her that it would be at least an hour and a half before I could get to the hospital since we lived over in Illinois. She seemed concerned that it would take that long. I could sense the urgent sound in her voice, the unspoken words hanging in the air: *Matt might not have that long.*

Pushing fear to the side, I told Bonnie I would get there as soon as I could.

"For in the day of trouble
he will keep me safe in his dwelling;
he will hide me in the shelter of his sacred tent
and set me high upon a rock."

(Ps 27:5) New International Version

DAY OF THE ACCIDENT

EVENING

After I got off the phone with Bonnie, I immediately called my daughter Nicole. I heard my voice, strangely calm, tell her what happened to her dad. I comforted her the best I could over the phone, though her crying stuck with me long after I hung up. The next frantic call was to my mom to tell her about Matt's accident. After telling her what I had been told, she helped me out by calling Matt's dad and his wife and asking them to please call Matt's mom and sister. I was frantic, but my mom helped to calm me down and told me to call Nicole back and ask her if I could pick her up on the way to the hospital. Once I had gathered some essentials for a few days, I headed to Nicole's house.

After getting Nicole, the miles disappeared under the wheels of my speeding car on my way to the hospital. Using the handsfree speaker, Nicole and I called Ryan, my son. He had graduated high school that past May and finished his senior season of baseball. At the end of July, he'd met with a coach and committed to playing baseball at John Wood Community College. That summer we'd moved him three hours from home and across the state.

Ryan picked up the phone on the first try and I told him, as I had Nicole, about what happened. I was extremely worried about calling him since his school was three hours from home and four hours from the hospital. I told him to sit tight until I could get to the hospital and find out more. It was still raining and storming across the Midwest, and I really did not want him driving in the weather. One person in the hospital was enough for this worried soul. I tried to be calm and make it sound like all was okay, but my children are perceptive.

"How bad is it?" he asked finally.

I took a deep breath and told him the truth.

The next hour, during the drive to the hospital, was a whirlwind of phone calls. I had Nicole hold the phone for me while I spoke with my colleagues, my principal, and friends, on speaker phone. I also needed to make sure things were taken care of at home. I had left the kitchen a mess from cooking and had left clothes everywhere when I had been packing. I hadn't cleaned up from Ryan being home that past weekend so there were messes everywhere. I needed to think about the pets, since I didn't when I left, and they were going to need to be fed. I also hadn't bothered to lock the house or shed and so I needed someone to run by home and take care of locking up and looking after the animals.

My mind was racing, but I kept saying to myself, *Lord you know what is best. You are my Savior and supplier of all my needs. Watch over us and help us get there.*

I convinced myself that if I was preoccupied during the drive, it wouldn't feel so long, but it still felt like an eternity. One of the routes to the hospital was the way Matt had likely been driving home and so I avoided that for fear of what I might see. I took a route that may have been a little longer, praying all the while that I wasn't making a mistake or that we would be too late. I sent up another prayer, *Lord, I am on my way, let me get there.*

Upon arrival at the hospital, Nicole and I charged into the emergency room to find out where Matt was. The instant we walked in, a stench of body odor filled the air. I could hear the anxious murmurs of others talking, the squeak of nurses' shoes on the linoleum floor, but the buzz of fluorescent lights gave me a steady calmness. We had to wait in line since there were others trying to check in. Though I was a nervous mess, it wasn't lost on me that each person was there for a reason just like ours. The emergency room was abuzz with men, women, and kids, all waiting for news on their loved ones. The woman in front of me in line was not happy and arguing with the check in nurse about them giving her son a Covid test. She didn't want to give in, and I wanted to shout over her head for the nurse to please tell me where my husband was. The seconds ticked by like a vice tightening around my chest. *What if this was Matt's last moment? What if* this *one was? Or the next?*

But I remained calm and waited my turn. Finally, I got to the front desk, asked about Matt, and the nurse directed us to the surgery waiting area. As we approached, we could see Matt's dad and his wife talking to a doctor. My legs could not move fast enough to find out how Matt was doing and what was happening.

The doctor speaking with my in-laws was named Doctor Lawson, and she was in the midst of drawing a diagram of Matt's injury on a scratch piece of paper. She was speaking very quickly, or perhaps I was in such shock that I couldn't make sense of her words normally. Dr. Lawson's brother was the lead surgeon on Matt's case, and they'd been working tirelessly to save my husband's life.

"The tree limb," she explained, "was originally six feet in length and had a diameter around three to four inches–the size of an adult fist. It pierced his chest, and broke his sternum at an angle all the way through and out the right side of his back." She pointed to the middle of the chest on her sketch and drew an arrow in the direction the limb had pierced Matt. "He broke many ribs," she continued, "not just broken, but shattered, which created holes in his lung. As many holes as possible were repaired and we removed the limb. Matt is stable, but extremely critical."

The air *whooshed* from my lungs. Stable. Matt was stable.

"My son," I said, after introducing myself to the doctor, "My son is at school four hours away. Should he come?"

"If you'd asked me that a few hours ago, I would have said to get your son here as quickly as possible," Dr. Lawson said. She had dark circles under her eyes, and I knew she'd been running for hours trying to save Matt's life. "But now that he's stable, your son can wait until morning." Then she told us that her brother, the lead surgeon, would be out once everything was complete.

Matt's Dad and I hugged and then we all prayed. Family is particularly important and at that time I was extremely thankful to not be there all alone. Our prayers were for Matt and the doctors. We prayed for healing and for God's will. I prayed silently to myself for God to give me the strength for my kids and Matt's family. I knew from that moment forward, I was going to need God more than ever while navigating this difficult situation. Since Matt was stable, I told Nicole to call Ryan and let him know he could wait for daylight tomorrow and for the rest of the storm to pass before getting on the road. She stepped away to a quieter area to make the call, but returned a short time later to report that Ryan was on the road already and would be at the hospital in two and a half hours.

After what seemed like an exceedingly long time, but was only about forty-five minutes, Dr. Lawson came out to explain the next steps. They had removed the tree limb, stabilized Matt, and he would remain in an induced coma. They would need to transfer him to a hospital in Indianapolis to undergo another surgery to repair his chest wall. There were two hospitals that could take him, but where he went would depend on which one had a bed available. They also had to wait until the storm and weather cleared to transport him via helicopter. In the meantime, he was admitted to the ICU. We could finally go up and see him.

There is very little in the world that can prepare a person for seeing their loved one in a hospital bed. In my mind, Matt was vibrant, lively, full of laughter and strength. The walk to his room was short but felt like an endless hallway as I waited to lay eyes on my husband. They'd put him in a private ICU room, but with glass-front doors. As the doors shut behind me, I suddenly felt like I was in a void—all the noise of the ICU outside was instantly muted and the quiet that fell over us was punctuated only by the sound of monitors beeping out a steady heartbeat. That was the only indication that the body on the bed was, in fact, alive. Matt appeared lifeless, and I staggered under the weight of emotions I'd been struggling to contain. The stark contrast of seeing vibrant liveliness stripped away from him as he lay in the hospital bed was overwhelming. He appeared peaceful, but seeing him lifeless and hearing the mechanical beeping and buzzing of machines that breathed for him was heartbreaking. I couldn't help it; I grasped my daughter's hand and burst into tears.

"You can sit with him," the nurse said to me, gently guiding me to a seat. I nodded, wiping my tears, and sat in the chair she provided. Nicole stood by my side, rubbing my shoulder as she looked at her father. Matt's chest rose and fell softly as the machines pumped air. His skin was cool and smooth where I held his hand.

His hand and parts of his face were the only visible parts of his body. He was wrapped in blankets from his shoulders to his feet, and his closed eyes were just visible between the tubes, wires, and straps holding them all in place on his face. I didn't want to imagine the wreck of his poor body underneath those blankets. I kept hearing the doctor describing the size of the branch that had impaled my husband—*about the size of a human fist.* A fresh wave of sobs gripped me.

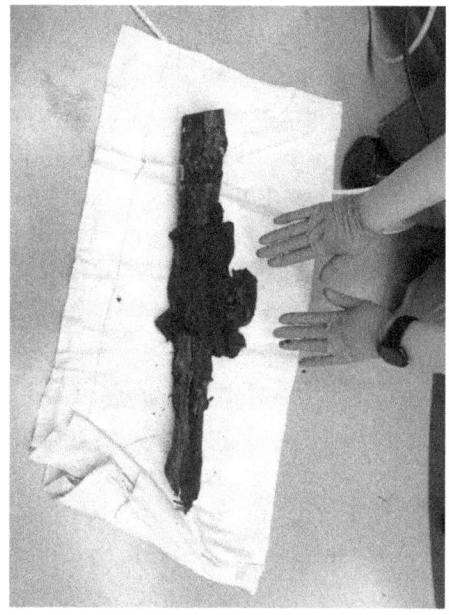

Tree limb that was removed from Matt's chest after several feet were cut off to fit him into the operating room.

They were waiting to hear about helicopter transport to Indianapolis. I could be with him until they arrived to prepare him to be moved. I gave him a kiss and then let Matt's father and wife take their turn to see him. After their visit, I went back to the room by myself and sat next to him and held his hand. Even though medical personnel were in the room, I was oblivious to their movements. All I could do was hold Matt's hand and talk to him so he could hear my voice. I wanted him to know I was there by his side, and I loved him. I cried, and I prayed, and I waited.

Eventually, I was notified that the helicopter had landed at the hospital, and I would need to go to the waiting room. I didn't want to leave. It had taken what felt like forever to be by his side and I didn't want to let go of my husband. However, they had a job to do and in order for Matt to heal and move forward, I needed to let them work.

In the waiting room, another nurse approached us with a plastic bag. "These are his things," she said, "What he was wearing and what he had on him at the scene."

"Thank you," I replied numbly. The nurse started walking away but turned back suddenly.

"Oh," she said, "Be careful when you take things out of the bag. There's still broken glass in there."

That was how my son, Ryan, found me as he rushed into the waiting area of the intensive care unit nearly half an hour later: sitting on the edge of a waiting room chair clutching the bag of clothes and glass. Ryan had made it right on time, to get a glimpse of his father as the helicopter crew passed by the waiting area with Matt less than hour later. The crew slowed down long enough for me to give him one more kiss with Matt on the gurney, and I said another silent prayer that everything would be okay.

As soon as they took Matt to the helicopter, we said goodbye to Matt's dad and his wife, shared a prayer, and discussed what would come next. Then, the kids and I drove to the nearest gas station to make sure the cars were filled with gas. Even though the drive was only a little over an hour, I wanted to make sure we all had the fuel we needed to get there and not worry about finding a place for fuel on the way. I had not been to this area of Indianapolis before and was apprehensive about the situation and finding out where Matt would be. I was alone on the drive since Nicole and Ryan rode together so Ryan could sleep. The quiet of the car made me feel uneasy; I finally had nothing to do or keep me busy but to drive. My mind wandered back to Matt, how he'd looked in the hospital bed, and what would happen next. I couldn't bring myself to acknowledge the question that sat, crouched in the back of my mind like a demon: would Matt survive this?

When I couldn't ignore the question any longer, I decided I needed to talk to someone about it. It was too late to call anyone, so I just talked to God.

Luckily, the storm that had so altered our lives hours before had dissipated, and the drive was smooth. The roads were empty; the weather was calm; it was as if God opened the path to make it easier for us to get to Matt. It wasn't until we arrived at the hospital in Indianapolis that we hit any kind of traffic and construction, so it took time to find the right parking lot.

Once inside, we made our way through the crowded waiting room to the check-in desk. The nurse verified that Matt had arrived already and was currently being attended to by the trauma team. We'd have to wait some more until we knew they'd be moving him to a room.

"You should get some rest, Mom," Nicole said as we got settled in a group of seats in a corner out of the way of the business. I patted her hand and smiled at her, but we both knew neither of us would really rest.

The busy waiting room made it difficult to relax and wait. Overlapping conversations drifted around us, punctuated by coughing, sniffling, and even crying.

I am not a person who likes the unknown. As a teacher, I valued planning, being prepared. So, it was doubly unsettling now to have no plan, no idea how to navigate the challenges I knew we'd face—and the challenges I couldn't begin to anticipate.

"Hey." I was roused from my thoughts by a gruff voice. I'd no idea how long I stared off into space, lost in my worries. The man who spoke was grizzly, with dirty nails and a scraggly unshaven face. "Hey," he said again, smiling at me. "I have a winning lottery ticket."

"Oh?" I asked. He held a slip of paper in his weathered hand which he proffered to me for examination. Even without closer inspection, I could see that it was a receipt of some kind, but definitely not a lottery ticket.

"Yeah," he said, his smile stretching wider. "I'll sell it to you."

"I'm...fine. Thank you."

"You sure?" The man wiggled the paper at me.

I sighed, opened my purse, pulled out a five-dollar bill. "Okay."

He finally left us alone. It is strange how everyday occurrences are so trivial compared to the grand scheme of life. I was facing some tough times ahead and yet I was trying to be gracious to a stranger in the ER. To him, getting that change for a snack was a huge deal, but for me it was not. Even in our worst of times, being mindful of others and what they're going through is important.

Finally, around 4:15 a.m., the nurse let us know that Matt was being taken up to the fourth floor. He would be in room 4212 of the Surgical Trauma ICU. Little did I know that was where I would be spending the next thirty-eight days of my life. We were given instructions on how to get to the front door and what to tell the attendant. I asked about our cars and the staff said we could leave them in the emergency room parking lot.

We made our way to the hospital front entrance, rang the bell, and explained to the attendant we had been sent over from the emergency room. She let us in and directed us to the elevators to go to the fourth floor. Once we arrived, our heavy feet and somber faces went to the door of the surgical trauma unit and rang the buzzer. No one answered.

Of course, after hours, we could not get in and no one was answering the buzzer. Finally, a medical staff person came along and checked with the doctor on call. She came out and told us they were still getting Matt settled and, if we could just wait a little, they would get us and take us back to see him. I was beginning to find new meaning in the phrase "hurry up and wait."

It was an exceptionally long hour with no waiting room, just a window ledge which we took turns perching on to relieve the ache in our feet and backs. I swore after this I would never again take for granted all the little things—a comfortable place to sit, a bed, quiet spaces, food, sleep. All things I didn't have enough of in the present moment.

When they finally let us in to see Matt, we tip-toed into his room as quietly as we could. He was resting, thank God, and none of us wanted to wake him. We found space in the small hospital room and slouched against the floor, the foot of his hospital bed, or just leaned against the wall, for as long as we could. The steady mechanical beeps of the various machines were the only sounds as we all rested the best we could.

Just prior to the shift change, we were told by the nurses that we had to leave so they'd have room to check on Matt's vitals. They didn't offer us chairs or say much of anything to us for those two hours. Once it reached the morning shift change around 7:00 a.m., we were told that only two people could return to Matt's room at a time. I didn't like that because there were three of us. I most definitely wanted to be always in the room and wanted Ryan and Nicole to be able to share time with their dad. But this was during the COVID-19 pandemic and rules needed to be followed. At least being in Indiana, they were less restrictive than Illinois and so all three of us were permitted to be in the hospital as long as only two people were in Matt's room at a time.

We headed to the hospital cafeteria to get some breakfast. We hadn't eaten in what felt like days, but even though we were hungry, none of us could summon a huge appetite. I had a few bits of toast and bacon, which were surprisingly good, and forced myself to have a cup of coffee and orange juice.

Keep your strength up, I kept telling myself. *We're going to need it.*

> *"Wait for the Lord;*
> *be strong and take heart*
> *and wait for the Lord."*
>
> *(Ps 27:14) New International Version*

DAY 1

From a sleepless night, Monday ran into Tuesday. The kids and I were tired, but we kept our rotation going so that two of us were with Matt at all times. Ryan and I were the ones in the room with Matt most of the day. That morning, the hospital chaplain came into the room. He asked me our religious affiliation and about our faith. I replied as succinctly as I could, but remember feeling so dazed that I'm not sure what I said made any sense. The chaplain noticed we were still in shock from the trauma of the previous day.

"May I pray with you?" he asked.

I instantly said, "Yes." After the prayer with us, he mainly tried to provide spiritual and emotional support. What was of the greatest concern to us and the hospital staff was that, even though he was sleeping, Matt was very agitated. Kelli, the nurse on his first day, tried to get him comfortable. She advised us not to touch Matt as most contact would likely make him very uncomfortable.

Collin, Nicole's husband, drove over to be with her. I found a hotel near enough to the hospital that we could get there quickly but would also have space for the four of us. We were in for the long haul with Matt's recovery, but there was no way we could spend it all cramped in his hospital room. The day was long, with all of Matt's immediate family there. His sister, Laura, and her husband John helped with all the cars.

"I'll move your car for you," John said, holding his hand out for my keys.

"Yeah," I said as I reached for my purse. "Thank you." I rummaged around for a few seconds, but didn't feel the familiar jingling of my keys against my fingers. I was in a panic as I couldn't find them. Nicole retraced our steps through the lobby to make sure I hadn't dropped them, and Ryan searched every corner of Matt's hospital room. In the meantime, John went to the emergency room parking lot and moved all the other cars to the hotel and proper parking. Not too long after he'd left, my phone buzzed in my pocket.

"Yes?" I answered, out of breath from searching for my lost keys.

"You can call off the search now," John said. I could hear a smile in his voice. "You left the keys in your car. Unlocked. Just waiting for me, I guess."

My breath *whooshed* from my lungs, and I collapsed into the chair, a smile slowly spreading across my own face. It was a welcome feeling. I chuckled lightly and John hung up to finish taking care of the cars. I looked at Matt, sleeping peacefully for once, his chest rising and falling gently. *Everything will be fine,* I thought. *Through God's protection, it will all be fine.*

⌒

That afternoon, I left the hospital for only about an hour, but Matt's family was there if the doctors needed anything. It was incredibly difficult to leave, not knowing what could happen in a blink of an eye. However, I got my family checked into the hotel, and I took a shower—my first in nearly two days—and then went right back. The kids stayed at the hotel, showered, and took naps. It was hard to see my children so distraught over their father; we each deal with calamity in our own way, and I had to work hard not to sink into mine, to remember that my children, though adults, still needed me. Matt needed me. This is something I'm not sure I appreciated about families that go through disaster situations like this: how tempting it is to forget about anyone else's pain but your own. The thought of losing my husband, my life partner, was crushing. But then, I remembered, my kids would lose someone dear to them, too. Loss is like that, I think—there's no telling how many people one single loss will touch. I had to remember that there was more to saving Matt than just how it would affect me. I shouldered my purse and left the hotel. There would be time to take care of myself later.

When I got back to the hospital, my family updated me on a meeting with a doctor I'd missed. The surgeon, they said, had done rounds shortly before I arrived at the hospital and probably wouldn't be back for some time. They told me Matt would have surgery on Wednesday to repair his chest wall. Before the surgery could take place, they needed to make sure Matt was strong enough and not running a fever. Also, it needed to be confirmed there was a room available for the long surgery.

"Does the community know?" my father-in-law asked at one point. "About Matt?"

"No," I sighed. I rubbed my face, massaging the bridge of my nose and hoping to relax the headache I could feel growing there. I knew I needed to get the word out and let people know about Matt. We'd have a lot of people in our corner sending up prayers for Matt, me and our kids. We have a dear friend in California who is a true prayer warrior. Anytime I have a big prayer request, I contact her. I made phone calls and then posted on Facebook letting friends and family know about Matt's accident. I became busy replying to messages from people praying and thinking of us. Messages offered help, prayers, and even disbelief.

When I texted my friend, Jenna, she immediately responded with, *What? Oh no! I am sorry, Jill. What is going on?*

Matt was driving and a tree fell on his car. This was the biggest understatement of my life, but I couldn't bring myself to share the full extent of my husband's injuries.

OMG, she replied. *He sure has some strange accidents. Do you need anything?*

I don't even know.

After a pause she asked, *Did they say he's stable now and it's looking good?*

I took a deep breath and typed back, my fingers shaking, *He is stable but critical. He'll be in the hospital awhile.*

I watched the three dots on my phone cycle back and forth as Jenna typed her reply. *Focus on Matt and your family. Please let me know if you need anything. I'm here always if you just need to vent, cry or talk! Miss you!*

Another friend, when I spoke to her on the phone, responded in disbelief. "Is it as bad as the first accident?" she asked.

"No," I sighed. I rubbed my eyes, exhausted. "It's worse."

In all of the hustle of the past days, I'd almost forgotten that our family had been through something similar nearly ten years before. In 2015, Matt was driving a ten-wheeler grain truck for his dad during the fall harvest. For some unknown reason, he ended up driving partially off the shoulder and, when he tried to get back on the road, the weight of the beans shifted the truck, and it rolled three times before stopping on its side with Matt inside the cab.

Matt's best friend happened to be on that road right after, found him still trapped in the cab, and called 911. Matt was airlifted to a local hospital and stayed for two days with a punctured lung, three brain bleeds, along with several broken ribs and collarbone. With the number of fractures and his type of injuries, the doctor said it was amazing he was alive. Not only did his recovery include seeing a specialist for an orbital fracture, but he also underwent surgery for an umbilical hernia about two months after the accident. *But Matt survived that,* I thought, *and surely God will look out for us and provide for us now.*

I said goodbye to my friend, hung up the phone, and continued calling.

By the end of the afternoon, we had prayers of support and healing from California to Florida, and many places in between. God could not help but hear the numerous prayer requests for Matt and his doctors and nurses.

Later that day, the trauma team treated Matt's fever with antibiotics. The staff wanted the best for the surgery, so they made sure he got rest to normalize his blood pressure. He was awake a little, so I talked to him to let him know Ryan and I were there.

By that Tuesday evening, everyone left Indianapolis except my children and me. Collin, Nicole, Ryan, and I went to a grocery store and got some food to take back to the hotel. At last, the hustle of the past twenty-four hours slowed, at least enough for us to begin processing. We ate in silence, the steady hum of the mini fridge the loudest thing in the room, as we finally let it all sink in.

It wasn't until then that I think I realized how tired I was. I had been awake for nearly forty hours, the adrenaline and pure terror the only things keeping me going forward. My eyes burned with exhaustion, and I thought for sure I would be able to sleep but, knowing that Matt's surgery was the next day, made it hard to sink into rest.

Instead, I listened to a song my brother sent me. Praise worship songs remind me that anything is possible with God. The song talked about all the wonderful works God does each day in people's lives.

The miracles that God performs are so good and show His love so completely that you must believe in Him. I remember listening to the song on repeat—there was something about the lyrics that soothed me, made the tightness in my shoulders and back ease, and made breathing feel easier. I fell asleep answering messages sent from friends across the country, sending us prayers and wishing us well. Their kind words and the song washing over me finally helped my eyes close. I slept and did not dream.

"You are the God who performs miracles:
you display your power among the peoples."

(Ps 77:14) New International Version

DAY 2

The next morning, we were up early to get to the hospital before the surgery. Once again, I missed a meeting with Dr. Pierce. I tried not to let the butterflies swarm in my stomach; meeting Matt's surgeon would have really put my mind at ease, but I was going to have to trust him sight unseen. Ryan and I went in to see Matt and waited until they were to take him down to surgery. There were not many words said between the two of us during that time, except for our short answers when the nurses came in to check on us.

As we sat and waited, all I could hear were the beeps and noises from the tube and monitors keeping Matt alive. My mom texted and asked me to call her when I had a free moment. I didn't have the heart to call her then; I didn't want to let go of Matt's hand.

When the nurses came to take him to surgery, I texted Nicole and told her to get everyone to meet us by the elevator. We all got to see him before I went with him down to surgery. Matt gripped my hand, though his eyes remained calm. He was still so tired, so broken, and my heart ached for him to have to go through this. One final prayer and I left the family to take Matt all the way.

I had to leave his side too soon as transport workers flocked around Matt's bed. One of them looked at me, her face covered by a mask. Her eyes were warm and reassuring.

"Just remember all the blessings," she said to me. I nodded but couldn't speak. "Remember all the blessings and trust in the good," she said again. And then Matt was gone.

No one really prepares you for feeling that powerless in the face of tragedy. As spouses, parents, friends, we often would do anything to alleviate pain for someone we love. To see my husband in such debilitating circumstances and knowing I did not have the expertise to help him—to really heal him—inspired a kind of anger at myself I didn't know I could feel. I needed to *act*. I needed to *do* something. But…there was nothing to do. Only wait.

I turned again to my praise songs, and Matt's family and I spent the hours of Matt's surgery mostly silent together, lifting up prayers for Matt, for his surgeons, for everyone who needed help fixing my broken husband. He had to pull through. He *had* to. He'd made it this far.

The day went so slowly as we waited for the surgery to be finished. Nicole had raved to Collin about the bacon and breakfast the day before, so we had breakfast. Ryan decided on a salad while I chose to have some fresh fruit. We just sat, talked, and prayed. During this time, I stepped away for a bit to call my mom. This was the first time I'd talked to her since I called the day of the accident. She picked up the phone on the first ring.

"Jill, honey," she said. The minute I heard her voice, I broke. I cried in the middle of the hospital courtyard, the catharsis of my own tears making me blind to everyone around me. I'd tried to hold everything down, to focus only on the practicalities of Matt's recovery and looking after my family. I wanted to be strong. I *needed* to be strong.

But my mother was someone I could let my guard down with. Sniffling, I found a quiet corner away from the bustle of the hospital café to finish my conversation with her.

"I don't know what to do, Mom," I hiccupped.

"You're doing exactly what you need to do. You're there for your kids. And you're there for Matt. That's all you need to do."

"What if he doesn't—" I couldn't bring myself to say the rest.

"You trust in God," my mother interjected, "You trust God and you believe your husband is strong enough to do this. Because he is."

Later that morning, Mark, a friend from Matt's home church in Illinois who lived near the hospital, came for a visit. By the time Mark found us, he was red-faced and out of breath; apparently, he'd walked around the hospital for quite some time looking for us. His nervousness did little to calm my nerves. Matt was still in surgery, and I couldn't stop myself looking at the clock to see how much time had passed.

I ended up doing the only thing I had control over in that moment: report cards. It had been so easy to forget that I had a life outside of this hospital, one that included school and students and grading. So, I dove back in and tried to sift through some assignments, and catch up on grading. It felt surreal to tackle something rather mundane, but there's nothing like waiting through a seven-hour surgery after a life-threatening accident with ordinary paperwork.

Work, however, was a known part of my life and Matt's out-come was not. Like most of us, I think, I do better if I know what's going on. Doing the reports cards sounds awful with what I was going through, but it gave me a focus for the day. After about five hours, Nicole and I went up to the surgery ward to wait. We were told they were closing him up and then Dr. Pierce would be out.

Ryan really needed to head back to school but wanted to wait to hear how the surgery had gone. Dr. Pierce was pleased; he could have continued to repair more ribs but had been in there long enough, and what he'd done would provide the support Matt's lungs needed. This was the first time I'd met him since I'd missed him the previous two times. Listening to him tell me the specifics of the surgery and how he'd repaired Matt's injury made me feel at ease, and as if everything was going to be okay. I let everyone know and hugged Ryan, then told him to drive safely and let me know when he made it back to school. I gave the team and nurses time to get Matt back to his room so that Nicole and I could see him. Just watching him sleep was so peaceful—yet also so hard to see such an active guy lying there restrained and unable to talk. I wondered if he knew what had happened. That night, alone in my hotel bedroom, I cried myself to sleep.

"Lord, hear my prayer,
listen to my cry for mercy;
in your faithfulness and righteousness
come to my relief."

(Ps 143:1) New International Version

DAY 3

Waiting and not knowing are two things I don't handle really well. That is exactly what the next few days after Matt's surgery were. Each morning, the trauma doctor and team made rounds. The first day after surgery, he was incredibly pleased with Matt's progress. Matt was able to breathe more on his own, so the breathing tube air was decreased. He managed to stay awake all morning and was lucid enough to really try to communicate with me. Communication was difficult still with the breathing tube in his mouth and down his throat. Jamie, the nurse for that day, helped tremendously by decoding what Matt was trying to tell us. She was a kind woman, light brown hair nearly always pulled back in a ponytail and glasses that winked in the hospital lights. She was soft-spoken and gentle and always seemed happy. I would come to rely on her smiles, on the positivity she brought to the room despite our immense struggles. Jamie worked with Matt to help him move and also to check his progress. While talking with her, I found out she grew up not too far from where we live. We were able to chat about home and it was nice to have a connection with her.

One of the first major hurdles for Matt, now that the worst of the surgeries was behind us, was to gain back lung function.

Matt fussed as much as he was able to, hating the ventilator and the various tubes connected to him, but the doctor patiently explained that he had to show us that he could breathe on his own.

Such a simple thing, I remember thinking. Breathing. Most of the time, it's so easy and automatic for us that we don't even think about the fact that we're doing it. And here was my husband, having to consciously prove that breathing was something he was capable of. Matt started breathing to try and show us he was strong enough. His gasping breaths worked against the ventilator, and he was not able to do it for an extraordinarily long time. He was not in pain, as he was on medication, but all the tubes he was hooked up to bothered him. The doctor watched closely and thought there was a possibility the tube could come out any time in the next few days.

He patted my arm on the way out of the room. Behind us, Matt was already sinking into sleep, exhausted from the effort of breathing. "This is good," the doctor said, "it's progress."

"At least we're making progress. You're right," I replied. In my mind, I was thinking we would be there for about a week.

Matt was in and out of sleep that entire day, the sound of the same constant rain of the past few days pattering on the window. Collin was returning home, hoping he and his dad could get in the field soon. His dad drove over to pick him up so Nicole would have her car when she wanted to go home. We also wanted to change rooms at the hotel because, with just Nicole and I, we didn't need the two-bedroom suite. We left Matt while he rested, to go back to the hotel, pack up all of our scattered things, and move to the second room. That evening, Nicole and I just ate the food we had back at the hotel. We talked about Matt's nurse, Jamie, that day and how she looked a lot like a teacher at school. We were able to smile, and it became a topic each time we saw Jamie. The days seemed long at the hospital, but the nights were even longer. I was not only physically tired but mentally drained. And I hated being away from Matt.

One of the things no one talks about when you're helping a loved one heal from a traumatic injury is the extent you'll go to in order to find anything to ease their pain. Which is what led me to sign Matt up for a music study. Two researchers come around and said that they were conducting a study on the effects of music on patients that were in the ICU for some time and how music plays a part in the patient's awareness and anxiety. I didn't think it could possibly hurt, so I said "why not?" After all, I knew Matt was still in terrible pain and, though he slept a lot, his discomfort was constantly etched across his features. Despite being in the hospital for days now, he still hadn't regained full awareness of what was going on, and couldn't talk me out of the study, anyway.

I thought some music in headphones for an hour or so each day wouldn't hurt. The researchers said the study would last for a few weeks and, after each music session, they would try to ask Matt a few questions. He'd go on to participate in this study for the duration of his stay in the ICU, but thinking back, I don't know how valuable it was for Matt to participate. While it didn't seem to add to his distress, half the time the researchers needed to ask him questions, he was in a heavily sedated sleep and the other half he was so agitated that he couldn't focus to respond to their questions. Those were the times I thought for sure he was going to be really mad at me.

Now, after the fact, I would not have agreed. This intrusion became a nuisance, and Matt was not very cooperative. It also went on even after he was released, when they called to do a final follow up. By that time, even though it was weeks later, we were trying to get back to work and to get on with our lives.

DAY 4

Day four in the hospital was October 15, 2021. Nicole and I got up and headed to the hospital after a quick breakfast. After just a few days, we were used to the drive and could easily navigate the parking lot and checkpoints of the hospital. Covid was still heavily present, so when we entered the hospital, we answered the standard Covid symptom questions and got a fresh mask for the day. The routine was to first check in at the nurses' station for any updates on Matt before we settled in Matt's room. Nicole and I would talk softly or watch videos on our laptops or phones. Most of the time, I just sat by Matt's side, held his hand, and prayed for God to help him get better. Sometimes, Matt was conscious enough to squeeze my hand back, or to give me just the faintest smile. It was those moments I held on to. They were proof that my husband was still in there.

That morning, though, around 11:00 a.m., Matt started showing some distressing signs. His morning had been good, but he was struggling with his oxygen. The doctors ordered an X-Ray to see what the issue was. The X-Ray didn't reveal anything significant, so they ordered a CT scan, too.

Hospitals are usually places where patience is the best virtue, but especially during Covid, the hurry-up-and-wait struggle tested me almost daily. While we waited for the CT results, I texted my family again, updating them on this potentially worrying change. I asked for added prayers for Matt's dad who was struggling to cope with the severity of Matt's injuries. He'd visited early that day and I honestly don't know if seeing Matt was helpful or harmful. I thought if Matt's dad could see him that it would help to know he was okay and at least improving.

I knew he had a lot of questions and, thankfully, our day nurse—a kind woman named Linda—answered them all patiently.

How long will he be this way?

When can the breathing tube come out?

Will he be back to normal soon?

That last question she didn't have a solid answer to. We were told again and again that we'd have to wait and see. More waiting. More seeing. But that is how the body heals, I suppose—waiting and seeing.

Finally, later in the day, we found out that fluid had built up around Matt's lungs, so his doctors planned to drain the fluid the next day. Even with that, Matt relaxed a little more over the course of the day and was able to decrease his ventilator use from 100% down to 60%.

This was a normal part of my vocabulary now. Trying to maintain normalcy when going through something devastating, shifts your perception of the word, I suppose. It never would have been normal to discuss oxygen use, fluid around the lungs, or CT scan results. But here we were, talking about it with the doctors as calmly as we could, making preparations for the next day with the same casualness that we'd plan out our Sunday trips to the grocery store after church. The most stressful thing of it all was keeping everyone else updated on Matt's condition. The truth was, sometimes there wasn't anything new to report. So, when people asked, I would say simple phrases like he was sleeping or resting because sometimes I just did not know what to say.

Nicole and I finally headed back to the hotel after a full twelve-hour day with Matt at the hospital. He was resting peacefully, and sleep was very much needed for the two of us. I was ready to sink my head into my pillow for a quiet night of rest.

"Consider it pure joy, my brothers and sisters,
whenever you face trials of any kind,
because you know the testing of your faith produces
perseverance."

(James 1:2-3) New International Version

DAY 5

After a night's rest, the morning of October 16 dawned chilly and clear. It was only five days into Matt's time in the surgical trauma ICU, but it already felt like an eternity. Matt was doing about the same and his doctor's top priority was just keeping him calm enough to rest. It wasn't uncommon, they told me, for patients on a ventilator to really struggle and get aggressive because it's horrible to have a tube shoved down your throat or up your nose. It's instinctive to want to take it out.

That morning, Nicole went home and Matt's dad and his wife also decided to stay home. I supposed it was coming—that eventually it would just be me and Matt together. I certainly didn't blame anyone. They had lives and homes and families to get back to as well. I chalked it up to the normal dust-settling after a catastrophe. The only difference, though, is that I was still living it.

Being alone with Matt in his hospital room was such a strange feeling. There was my husband in the bed, and yet...not my husband. Not completely. The accident had taken away so much of him that I knew it would be ages before we'd act and talk and laugh together like we always had. The constant beeps of his machines and the hiss and whir of his ventilator were the only noises in the room for a good portion of the day. I was dimly aware of the ambient alerts, buzzers, and all-calls outside our room, but the world of the hospital might as well not have existed. I forgot that the world kept going on around us.

Every so often, a nurse would pop her head in or a doctor on his rounds would come in to check the monitors and check for atelectasis, hypoxemia, and any other physiological changes, but for most the day I was alone. As the sun started to set that day, I realized it was the first time I'd spent a whole day alone with Matt since his accident. And he'd pulled through all right. So had I. I was both uneasy and relieved at the same time. I'd always had someone there to talk to or eat lunch or supper with. Someone else to share the quiet and stressful situations. But it was also nice to be able to be myself without holding back. I could easily relax and not worry about having to be strong for others. That day I let myself cry while holding Matt's hand. I let myself feel despair and hope and even anger.

Selfishly, I mean gosh, I wanted everyone to stop what they were doing and give me sympathy. But at the same time, I wanted none of that because I didn't want to bother others. My life consisted of getting up, going to the hospital, and sitting for hours. I'd break for lunch then sit for more hours, then decide when it felt right to leave and get dinner and try to sleep. I felt guilty when I wasn't by Matt's side, not in his room watching him sleep or breathe, but also felt bored and helpless, like I was doing absolutely nothing and even getting in the way without meaning to.

There were three different doctors that kept coming in to check on Matt. Each doctor had their perspective and what they wanted to do. Two disagreed a lot so I really didn't know what the concrete plan was, since they offered different advice at different times.

One doctor wanted to pull Matt's breathing tube out and wanted to do certain things as far as meds. The other doctor wanted to wait on removing Matt's tube and talked about a possible tracheotomy. It was difficult to navigate their advice—one was a very aggressive treatment approach and the other was more conservative. Not being a medical expert, obviously, made it challenging for me to know which were the right decisions.

Later that evening, I called my dad. It was good to hear him and have a simple conversation. Sometimes, just hearing the voice of someone can help to ease your fears. I ended the evening feeling somewhat eased; while the treatment options were opposites of each other, my father reminded me that they had Matt's care in mind at all times. My choice couldn't be wrong. I had to trust the team. And I had to continue to trust my intuition.

DAY 7

During the doctors' rounds in the morning of October 18, our seventh day in the STICU, Doctor Gray was genuinely concerned about how Matt was doing.

"There is a chance," she told me, "That Matt will develop a threatening condition called hypoxic respiratory failure. In cases like that, he will require more medical ventilation, which we want to avoid."

"What would that mean?" I asked.

"Well, right now, it just means that we observe every hour how he's doing. We want to avoid the circumstance that Matt's body and brain aren't getting enough oxygen because of a sudden failure of his lungs. Remember, he's still working incredibly hard to breathe on his own after the damage his chest cavity endured."

"Sure," I said, nodding. Just when it felt like Matt was making progress, something else worrisome reared its ugly head.

"We also need to monitor his recent fever," Dr. Gray said. Matt's fever had spiked earlier that morning and so he'd been quickly placed on antibiotics; he'd been awake for only a little of the time, but the rest of the meds were still being delivered intravenously.

"We're doing all we can," Dr. Gray continued, "And I know

you're doing everything to be there for him, too. Keep doing what you're doing."

Dr. Gray left us, and I returned to my seat by Matt's bed. The lights in the room were dimmed, the curtains drawn closed around us. Again, I felt like we were in our own little world. I wanted to return to *our* world, though. Our life.

I thought about how just last month we'd traveled to Ryan's school to watch him play some baseball games. Ryan had been adjusting well to living on his own, though Matt and I missed him terribly now that we were officially empty nesters. We'd spent the weekend laughing together and admiring how our son was teaching himself "adulting" tasks—how to cook and do laundry, and learning to live in a house with three new roommates.

My children had always been right with me and now one was married, and the other was moved out and far away. I started school again and Matt was traveling a lot for work. Our kids were gone, and we were apart. This was an extremely hard transition in our lives. I remember evenings just sitting in silence, pondering how hectic life had been. One night, while Matt was away for work, I just sat lost in the quiet of the living room, while my mind swept in and out of the memories. It was a bittersweet mix as I relived the moments both joyous and poignant all at once, for all the blessings God had brought my way.

The shrill beep of the medicine monitor roused me from my daydream. It was time to change the bag and I looked at the steady drip of Matt's IV. My thoughts returned to the hospital, to this room, to this horrid chair, and my husband's mangled body. A nurse came in promptly, stepping around me to grab a fresh IV bag and to check over Matt's vitals.

For a moment, we both stood and looked at Matt in silence, at the steady rise and fall of his breathing.

"It's like the tortoise and the hare, isn't it?" I commented absently.

"Slow and steady wins the race," the nurse finished. "He may not be out of the woods, but he'll get there."

If Matt could just breathe slowly and steadily more on his own, he would be able to get the tube out. I was encouraged that he seemed a little more awake and coherent that day, but he was always hot so the nurses set ice packs around him. Matt constantly kicked off his sheets and complained of being hot. The room was hot. The covers were hot. The pillows were hot. I wanted to tell him there wasn't anything I could do about it, but how could I when he was so covered in wires and tubes, fighting for life at every turn?

He and I practiced his breathing before I left the hospital for the night. He asked if he was doing good by giving me a thumbs up. I told him yes and he gave a little smile. I rubbed his arm gently; that he could smile now made my heart happy to see. The past few days had been exceedingly difficult. He was awake enough to ask when we could go home, and could even say "let's go," but he was no way well enough to even be thinking about going home. While I know it disheartened him that he couldn't leave the hospital, I was encouraged that he could voice that want. What's more, after a week of the hospital, he *finally* was aware of me in the room and wanted me to stay with him.

Once I left the hospital for the night, I stopped and picked up orange chicken and fried rice for dinner and went back to the hotel. I spent the evening trying to just relax. While sitting and eating, I read through my messages. The days were usually so busy that, even with my mind churning, I normally fell into a deep sleep fairy quickly, but that night I had a very uneasy feeling about Matt. After I spent some time listening to praise music and praying, I finally called in and asked to speak to his nurse. They said she was busy, and they would have her call me back. Concerns ran through my head, but I had to remind myself that there were other patients and that her being busy had nothing to do with my husband. Later, with heavy eyelids that wanted sleep, they called me back, they said Matt had tried to get out of bed and had pulled his catheter out. He had to be put on a higher dose of medicine to calm him down so he wouldn't harm himself.

DAY 8

The next morning, Nicole and I got up late to get to the hospital. I wasn't sure what I would find after last night's escapade with Matt and the catheter after trying to get out of bed. His fever was down a little, though he had grown agitated again and tried to take out his catheter a second time. He'd been taken to test if he had caused any damage, but everything checked out okay. Around mid-morning, Matt grew irritated again, and doctors and nurses alike worked to find the cause. Mostly, and very understandably, the tube in his mouth made him feel uncomfortable. He would try to bite it out of frustration but then have to let go because the oxygen couldn't get through. The nurses attached a clip to the tube so he couldn't bite down. He kept trying to move the tube to the side, thinking he could push it out of his way. Luckily, his hands were restrained, or my guess is he would have pulled that out too.

Just to be diligent, however, the team of nurses checked for other causes for his irritation. He rested a lot but that was because they had him on pain medicine and also calming medicine. I felt torn between wanting him to wake up so we could talk and wanting him to sleep so he'd remain calm and not damage the tubing and IVs. When he was awake, though, Matt was very indecisive—first he needed me to cover his feet, then take the blanket back off, then put it back on again. Then he asked me to take him home. I smiled sadly and told him neither one of us would go home for a while.

That same wave of helplessness crashed over me again. I just wanted him back. I wanted him to be able to speak with his voice and not motions. However, Matt and I were getting better at our new communication—I'd ask yes or no questions and he'd respond and follow commands with a thumbs up and a squeeze of my hands when nurses asked. He also communicated by kicking his legs on the bed when he wanted something.

Each day that week, Dr. Gray and the trauma team suggested doing a tracheostomy. They saw his breathing improving, but with every step forward there was another step back. The tube had been in a while and was nearing the maximum number of days patients were recommended to have a tube through their mouths. The trach would require Matt to undergo local anesthesia to move the tube from his mouth to a hole in his throat. This was hard for all of us. I asked about the reasons why and what would happen if we did not do a trach. Dr. Gray and her team were adamant about the trach and suggested a family conversation to talk over the options.

The past week had been full of things I never thought I would have to talk about with my family, and this phone call was no exception. So, that evening when Nicole and I left the hospital, we called Ryan and the three of us had a family conversation about the trach. We came to the agreement that we knew it needed to happen, even if other people felt we should wait. The doctor felt it was necessary, and we trusted her expertise.

Wednesday, October 20 was a good day for Matt. He was relaxed and asked for his face and feet to be scratched and then asked for a hug. Nicole and I did a group call with Matt's family to discuss the trach being put in sometime in the next few days. This was hard for me, but I had notes talking about the reasons for the trach and that looking at the best interest for Matt and what he needed to move forward. The good news from that day was that Matt's left chest tube was taken out since it was no longer needed. One tube of many gone, but we both were encouraged at the positive direction. During my conversation with the family, I start with the good news. That really broke the ice. I then led into the trach being put in. I followed my notes and talked about the positives and that the two kids and I agreed and that it would be done. It went well and I felt like the family understood and were supportive.

DAY 10

The next morning, Thursday, October 21, was the day the surgeons planned to remove the breathing tube from Matt's mouth and do a tracheostomy in his room at his bedside, but we were still incredibly nervous about this procedure. I understood rationally that hospitals and doctors do procedures like this daily. However, emotionally, it seemed very scary to me that they would put a cut in Matt's throat to insert a tube without putting him fully under anesthesia. All I could do at that point was trust in God and that He would be there guiding the doctors and staff.

Later that afternoon, the team removed the right chest tube. I saw this as a particularly good sign of improvement. This meant Matt did not have any fluid buildup, and we could continue to move forward on the road to recovery. Maybe we would not need to do the tracheostomy if his breathing improved.

"For I know the plans I have for you,' declares the Lord,
plans to prosper you and not to harm you,
plans to give you hope and a future."

(Jer 29:11.) New International Version

DAY 11

With each procedure or surgery performed, the hospital required a signed consent form. After the fourth or fifth consent form, I felt like buying a house was a simpler paperwork trail. Of course, I wanted any procedure that would help Matt, so I signed each time. However, sometimes when I signed a document, especially if it was a more aggressive form of treatment, I couldn't escape the nagging question of "Is this the right thing?" that inevitably needled the back of my mind. This was especially difficult after every conversation regarding the risks of the procedure. Of course, every surgery has risks. You can't cut into the human body and expect nothing potentially harmful to come of it. But that didn't stop my hesitancy and the reminder of the old adage that "the devil you know is sometimes better than the devil you don't."

On day eleven in the ICU, I signed another form, this one for Matt's tracheostomy. We waited all morning with Matt, knowing that he would likely be exhausted and sleeping after the procedure. I wanted to spend as much time in the room with him as I could.

When Doctor Gray came in, finally, she carried a tray of surgical implements with her. I tried not to eye the sharp scalpels and wads of gauze as she asked us to go to the waiting room. She'd need a little over an hour and promised to come get us as soon as it was done.

Nicole and I went to the fifth floor waiting room and settled in two chairs. She started to do some work, and I checked on things for school. After a truly brief time, the doctor came in. I jumped out of my chair, surprised to see her so soon.

"You're done already?" I exclaim.

"Well," Dr. Gray began, rolling her eyes, "Matt didn't respond well to the trach."

My stomach sank, a hot acid building up in my gut. The worst scenarios flashed through my mind.

"He's stable now," Dr. Gray said, "but when we gave him the local anesthetic his oxygen dropped, and his heartrate changed more than we were comfortable with. I wasn't okay with the severity of his reaction to the meds, so I chose not to continue. This happens sometimes, but it's not what I wanted with Matt's course of treatment. The breathing tube really does need to come out."

"Well," I said, willing my voice not to shake, "I'm relieved that you stopped if it was really worrying."

"I agree. We'll need to monitor him before we try again. His stats are up now, and he's stable. I want to try again, but we'll have to see how he handles the anesthetic leaving his system."

Nicole and I returned to Matt's room. Not quite an hour later, his heart rate and blood pressure were not doing so well. There was also a return of a slight fever, so he was sent for a CT scan, after they took some x-rays. The results from the x-rays did not show anything but he was still not bouncing back from the attempt to do the trach. I felt so confused as to what was wrong with Matt. I couldn't shake the thought of every potential disaster playing out in my head.

As the worst thoughts crept into my mind, all I could do was pray. *Dear Lord, watch over Matt. Help him to control his anxiety and bring his oxygen and heart rates back to normal.*

Maybe, I thought, *this is a sign that a trach isn't necessary.* After all, if he wasn't able to get it done maybe that meant he was healing on his own. This thought really brightened my day and would have helped his whole family feel so much better. But then the CT scan was cancelled after a few hours as he was starting to get back to normal. They were trying not to put him through anything unless absolutely necessary. Matt sure was giving the medical staff a workout that day and part of me was happy to see a little energy and fight coming back to him. I'm sure the hospital staff slept well that day, after dealing with him.

Later that afternoon, Matt's team decided that he had trouble tolerating procedures; therefore, they planned do the tracheostomy in the operating room the next day. I felt a little relief that at least the surgery would be done in an operating room rather than his hospital room but worry still remained wedged deep in my heart.

I did not have much experience dealing with day-in and day-out trauma. Putting it simply, hopefully many people do not have to deal with going through such trauma anyway, but each day now made me look back on my life before Matt's accident and realize how *good* it truly was. God had treated us well. But now, each day for almost two weeks, I'd sat by Matt's bedside, talked with the nurses, and went through motions of "being there." Physically, I was present each and every day but, in my mind, I was horribly scattered. Many times, I tried to focus on things outside of Matt and the hospital—things I had control over. I continued to update my class page for my students and upload assignments and messages for them. I was also in contact with another teacher who planned to be in Indianapolis over the weekend, who offered to bring all my papers so I could look at them, grade them, and send them back to school. It's the little things, I realized, that were going to get me through the day. The big issue—getting Matt well—was something I had to trust in the doctors and God for. The bigger plan was something I could observe, but not necessarily do anything to change. His body and his mind just needed the time. The little things, though, paperwork and text messages— things that I could attend to immediately, did wonders to give me daily purpose and focus outside of being with Matt.

DAYS 12 - 14

The twelfth day of Matt's hospital stay was the new trach day. When I got to the hospital, Matt was back to low blood pressure and low heart rate, which meant he wasn't in the best place for attempting the procedure. But I knew that at some point the doctors were going to have to attempt the trach; too much time on a ventilator tube causes scaring and irrevocable damage to vocal cords.

The morning rounds with the doctors and nurses were getting quicker, but the doctors were still trying to figure out effective ways to keep Matt calm and relaxed and not to get him agitated. After monitoring him and his stats for several hours, they felt he was stable enough to go to the operating room. By the time they made that decision, though, there was already a wait for an open and ready OR.

My mother, who wanted to be with me, but couldn't, sent me a text that morning. *Just another reminder of hospital life*, she said while sitting at a different hospital with my dad, *hurry up and wait.*

I smiled thinly as I texted back. *I want a different life.*

By midafternoon, Matt was finally taken to the OR to put in the trach. I was a basket of nerves waiting to hear how the procedure went. It took around an hour. When the doctor came out to tell me about the surgery, he said Matt responded just like yesterday and they'd gone ahead and proceeded with the surgery. My heart dropped, knowing that they'd pushed ahead with the surgery given their concerns from last time.

"Not to worry," the doctor said quickly. My face must have betrayed me and revealed the calm I was trying to show. "While his oxygen level did drop some, we were able to keep going with the procedure. He was a little agitated, but thankfully now he's sleeping, and his oxygen levels are back where we want them."

The breath *whooshed* out of me. "Thank you," I said. I shook the doctor's hand and was left, alone again, with Matt in his hospital room.

After a while in any place, it's normal to get comfortable with the routine and the people around you. By the second full week of Matt's stay, I found myself completely at home in the hospital wing. I chatted with the nurses as if we were old friends, asking about their children or their holiday travel plans. I'd seen patients come and go from the rooms around Matt, their family members all equally excited to take their loved ones home. Each time I saw this, I felt a pang of envy, imagining the day that I'd be able to take Matt home, too.

Then, on day fourteen, Matt asked me where he was and how long he'd been there. His eyebrows went up when I said ICU in Indianapolis. I'll admit to being a little surprised at his confusion—there were moments in the previous days where he'd seemed lucid and aware of his surroundings, but the fact that he asked now only spoke to the depth of his injuries...and the strength of his painkillers. He kept asking when he could go home, like a child's refrain, "How much longer?" It broke my heart—and his, I think—to tell him we were still a long way away from being able to leave.

He even asked me to cut his restraints. Though he couldn't comfortably speak yet because of the trach, he used his hands to show me scissors cutting the ties of the arm restraints. I tried to explain to him, to fill in the gaps, that because he'd been in so much pain, anxious, and agitated, he needed restraints to prevent him from doing further harm to himself. Frown lines furrowed Matt's brow and he continued to be adamant that we remove his restraints.

I couldn't remove them without hospital staff, so Jamie—who'd visited often during our stay since that first day and who'd become a very appreciated presence in our lives—came in and explained again that he couldn't have his restraints off. But she did take some time to untie him and move his arms and legs to give him a break from time to time.

While I was grateful for this, it did little to relieve Matt's immediate frustration. He often complained about things the nurses would have to come help him with. After the trach was put in, he no longer complained about the ventilator tubing, but instead the line in his nose that was meant for nutrition.

I sighed and recalled a verse a friend sent to me earlier that day:

Be joyful in Hope,
patient in affliction and faithful prayer

(Rom 12:12).

DAY 14

The trach remained in, despite Matt's objections to it. He still slept a lot and woke up slowly, the drugs receding and advancing in his system like waves. When he was more awake, though, I started to see traces of my husband coming back. He asked questions, commented on things around him, even said hello to the nurses. But still, he could not get comfortable.

There were two questions everyone always asked: they wanted to know if Matt was breathing on his own, and they wanted to know when he'd be able to go home. The first question I could answer pretty easily. No, he wasn't yet breathing completely on his own. The second question—only God knew. That was my answer almost every time. *Only God knows.*

Sometimes the constant questions that I did not have answers to really ate away at me. They felt like acid, melting away every piece of strength I had. I'd build up a foundation of surety only to have another curveball in his treatment plan to overcome. I just wanted this situation to have a plan and to be resolved. Even though Matt couldn't articulate it, I knew he must have felt the same way.

The evening of the fourteenth day of Matt's recovery, I woke up from my doze in the chair in Matt's hospital room to a text message from my mother.

How did your day go?

Crazy, I replied, *just crazy. Matt can't calm down and when he's awake he's confused and asks questions I don't have answers to.*

What questions?

He's so out of it, he keeps asking me why he's here. I tell him he's hurt and his lungs need to heal, but every time he wakes up he acts like he's ready to go.

Bless his heart.

The doctors keep giving him meds to calm him down. I can't begin to tell you the number of drugs they're pushing into his system.

It's a Catch-22, my mother replied. *With medicine, you can take it for one thing, but they always have side effects that cause other problems.*

I looked at Matt where he lay sleeping in bed, the IV lines still connected to the tops of his hands and arms. *Tell me about it,* I texted back.

Trying to manage Matt's pain and his pain meds was proving to be a vicious cycle, a merry-go-round we couldn't get off. Every day, he woke up and saw the exact same room, the exact same people, unable to move. After a while, I think anyone's mind would play tricks on them. Time would feel too fluid ... or time wouldn't feel like anything at all. The disorientation of it was maddening and I didn't blame Matt for feeling so frustrated and being so—at times—belligerent.

How are lungs doing? My mom asked.

It's just a matter of time, I tell her. It's a little too complicated to explain over a text message that when Matt was in surgery to repair his chest wall, they had to remove a similar part of the lung as they do for cancer patients. His lungs were smaller, weaker, struggling to adjust. It takes time for the organs to "relearn" how to breathe with what's left. As always, the doctor seemed hopeful. But we still weren't ready to leave the Intensive Care Unit.

The days blurred together as I tried to stay on top of messages, updates, and family threads. An added hassle presented itself when I had to deal with the issue of my hotel room. I had only reserved the room for twelve days and here we were at two weeks and no end in sight. I tried to extend my hotel stay, but there were no rooms available Tuesday, Wednesday, and Thursday at my current hotel. I kept asking in case of potential cancellations. I finally realized from watching the news that the National FFA convention was in town.

I didn't relish the thought of leaving Matt, but not being able to find a room was the push I needed to go home. I'd been away so long that I shuddered to think of the condition of the house, the spoiled food in the fridge, the mail that must have piled up. Not to mention I needed paperwork for our car insurance, and I missed our dog and cats (who'd been well-looked after in the meantime, but I still missed them). All these things were trivial, but since I did not have anywhere to stay, it was good timing.

I'm not sure it's possible to describe how surreal it was to drive home without Matt. The car was quiet and, unlike my first trip to the hospital, I didn't have anyone's company to talk me through the miles; no phone ringing, no text message alerts. The weather was calm and sunny. The nagging worry at leaving Matt stayed curled in my belly like a python, but there was something lighter about being out in the world and away from the hospital. I wished that Matt could have been well enough to make the drive with me. By no means, though, did I take it easy that evening.

By the time I got home, the sun was setting, but I worked

long into the night getting things squared away, washing clothes, cleaning, and running around. My dear friend and former teacher partner, Kris, came out after she got off work. She just talked with me and brought me a care package from her and some of her coworkers. The basket was full of soda, coffee, muffins, cookies, snack mix, gum, pasta packets, canned meat, and bagels. Nicole and I would be set with breakfast food, dinners, drinks, and snacks for several days. There was also a card with money inside to help with expenses.

My eyes filled with tears at such generosity and my friend hugged me until my sobs subsided. Amid tragedy, human goodness really shines through.

After my friend left for the night, I collapsed into my own bed, relishing in the simple luxury of it. My dog and cats curled around me, comforted at my return. Life, for a second, felt almost normal. If it wasn't for the empty space in our bed where Matt should be.

The next morning, I drove back to Indianapolis and into the familiar hospital. Matt was resting. During the doctor's rounds, our new doctor for the week, Dr. Cox, showed me the X-ray of Matt's lungs from the first day and the one from now. I liked Dr. Cox immediately; he was so down-to-earth and willing to give me the time to talk about Matt's recovery in detail. His gentle approach and the care he gave us is something I've never forgotten.

Not only will I always remember his gentle approach, but that it was he who showed me those first encouraging X-rays. I was amazed at the change and improvement between the pictures. I learned that there were three lobes on the right lung and two lobes in the left; the two smaller lobes from Matt's right lung had been removed. Also, the X-ray showed how battered and damaged the lung was from the first day to now. I was so glad to be able to see the actual healing and change. Progress really was happening, despite the days that felt like this would be our life from here on out.

Overall, things were looking up that whirlwind week. By Thursday, Nurse Jamie had Matt sitting in a chair first thing in the morning. He was already in the chair by the time I got to the hospital and had fallen asleep, but at least he was up. He'd had a good night, and the nurses were able to decrease some of his IV meds. I saw it as making progress. This was one of the happiest times so far during this traumatic event. Jamie had even taken Matt's restraints off again and given him some freedom of movement. When I updated his family, they were ecstatic.

Matt's chair, as I came to call it, was not a normal overstuffed recliner; it was specifically designed to accommodate the various tubes and wires of a patient in the ICU. Because Matt was still connected to so many machines, moving him from the chair back to his bed was a process that took time—and at least four people!

That first day in the chair, he was able to sit comfortably for a few hours, but when it came time to move him back, he started having a panic attack. Nurse Jamie was able to calm him down eventually, and I realized that when they moved him anxiety was the only way he responded. It was too much for him to bear, but to move forward he needed to keep battling the anxiety of getting up and moving around.

Later, he felt better and, for the first time, he was able to have a physical therapist come into the room to work with him. Since he'd spent so long lying in bed, restrained and not allowed to move, giving him a workout would be good. I think the more they moved him the better he would be each time. That afternoon, Matt was doing well, and the therapist was pleasantly surprised at his strength. The therapist did a few exercises with Matt and asked him if he wanted to get up. Of course, Matt was ready to jump out of bed without delay. However, the therapist said he would be back in the morning to get him out of bed.

As with most recoveries, for every step forward a half step back was inevitable. That evening, Matt mouthed asking me again if it was time for us to leave.

"No, Matt," I said. "We can't leave."

He got so mad he slumped back in bed and looked away from me, ignoring my looks and explanations. In my own frustration I said, "fine," gruffly handed him the TV remote and the call button for Jamie, grabbed my bag, and headed for the door.

"Wait," he managed to get out through the trach from the bed. His voice was tinged with sadness, and I turned to face him. There were tears in his eyes. He patted the bed and looked at me longingly as if to say, "I'm sorry. I don't know why I said that. I'm sorry, Jill."

I sighed, the fight leaving me as I saw my husband struggling to rein in the feelings of helplessness that I knew all too well. I put my things back down and stayed. In my heart I felt bad, but I was dealing with so much stress and if he didn't want to cooperate, I did not need to be there. I knew he didn't really mean it and that as he got better, he'd likely feel more and more frustrated with the pace of his recovery. After a while, I said it was time for me to go, and I was able to smile and pat his hand while a smile flicked across his face, his eyes already closing to sleep.

"And now these three remain: faith, hope and love.
But the greatest of these is love."

(1 Cor 13:13) New International Version

DAY 18

The eighteenth day of our stay was a day I will always remember. The previous one had been so good—Matt was proving to the physical therapist that he was getting stronger. The therapist was encouraging and happy that he was so willing to challenge himself a little more each day. Motivation, the therapist explained, was key with recoveries like this, which were often long, painful, and frustrating. The therapist agreed that he was probably ready to stand up and start trying to walk around.

When the time came, several nurses, including a respiratory therapist named David and a nurse named Elanor, helped to get Matt up. However, Matt was not as strong as they thought and was not able to completely get up and walk like they'd planned. So together, they got him to sit up on the bed, stand up, and then turn around to sit in the normal chair I'd been sitting in for the past weeks. It was such a moving moment, but it came to a devastating halt moments later.

Matt was sitting in the chair, and I tried talking with him, but he seemed very uneasy. I felt like no matter what I did to try and help him, he just could not get comfortable. He asked me several times to get the nurse to put him back in bed. I tried to explain they wanted to keep him out of bed and in a chair for at least an hour, since it was a lot of work to get him up. He said he felt nauseous. I called for Elanor, and she gave him a shot to alleviate the nausea, but he still could not relax. He was fidgety and wanted a bucket. It took several times of him telling me before I figured out what he wanted. Then I began looking all around the room for some type of bucket to let him have under his chin. He would not hold it, so I stood and tried to hold it. He became extremely frustrated. He began gagging like he was going to vomit. So, I got the tub under his chin again. David was in the room, monitoring his breathing, and asked if he needed to get the nurse for something more for nausea. I said I thought they'd already given him all they could.

Matt and I went round and round for what felt like forever. Bucket, then no bucket. Sick, then not sick. Gagging and then coughing. I hated seeing him confused and suffering. I just wanted the hour to be over. During one of the times where he felt really sick and was gagging and coughing, I happened to take the tub away from under his chin and noticed that the trach had come out. There had been times before where the outer part resting on his skin would push out and the nurses would pop it back on, but this was different. The whole apparatus was out farther than I'd ever seen before, so I asked David to look at it. He tried to just pop it back in but had no luck. He called Eleanor, another respiratory therapist, and an intern.

I sat there, watching in disbelief, as they all worked to try and get the trach back into its proper place. This wasn't working, and I stood there helpless, listening to my husband say it hurt and watching as the intern grew more frazzled wondering why he couldn't push it in. He called Dr. Cox, and when he arrived, he decided they needed to lean Matt back to try and get the trach repositioned that way. Still no luck.

Then Dr. Cox asked me to leave the room. I absolutely didn't want to, but obeyed because I knew it meant they were going to have to try a more drastic measure to get the trach placed. It was torture to stand in the hallway and watch them all struggling to get Matt comfortable. I just stood outside the room, totally in a fog but listening as I heard snippets of conversation.

"We need to get him back in bed."

"He needs to be laying down."

"He's lost his airway."

And then Matt whimpering, "This hurts, please help!"

I bit the inside of my cheek until it hurt, willing myself to stay in the hallway instead of charging into the room to demand they stop hurting Matt. Over the next few minutes, the hall outside of room 4212 became a meeting point. There were doctors, nurses, respiratory support, a social worker, the chaplain, and a man in a white coat who I didn't recognize. I assumed the man in the white coat was another doctor, perhaps a specialist they'd called in, but I found out later that he was a hospitalist who drops in when "the end is near." If I'd known that then, I surely wouldn't have continued waiting in the hallway.

The man in the white coat stood inside the doorway and I heard him ask, "Is this for real?"

"Yes," came the reply. Moments later, the intercom crackled to life and announced words I never want to hear again.

"Code blue, room 4212. Code blue."

Matt's room. Right on the other side of the wall from where I stood. My heart sank and my whole body trembled. A code blue meant that the patient was in cardiac arrest and wasn't breathing.

I looked at the ceiling, tears brimming in my eyes as more

doctors and nurses bustled around me. *Please God,* I prayed, *we've come so far. Please not now.*

For several minutes, which felt like hours, I heard things from Matt's room. I sat on a stool, just outside the room at an alcove where nurses can write notes. Everyone in the room was working frantically to bring Matt back. They had moved him from his chair to his bed, given him CPR and replaced the trach.

"Where's the wife?" I heard someone ask.

"She's in the hall."

I heard others ask for supplies. A cart had been placed just outside the door full of supplies to resuscitate patients, give them an airway, and help make them comfortable. The social worker asked if she could call someone for me, but I couldn't process anything at the time. I just ignored her help and felt bad later that I had been so passive. I had never met her, and she was not being intrusive, but was just trying to do her job.

Up to that time in the hospital, I hadn't cried in front of other people. I had kept my composure, especially for my children, but also because I did not like crying in front of others. There was no stopping the tears this time. I was handed some Kleenexes and asked if I wanted to go to a private room. I shook my head. No way was I leaving that spot while it was possible my husband was taking his last breath.

My family and I have always trusted that things are in God's time and that when He says it is your time to go to Heaven, He will call for you. But I just could not believe that God would take Matt now, after all the trauma we'd already gone through. I was dimly aware that the chaplain was trying to divert my attention from what was going on by asking questions about Matt and our family. I was polite and answered but kept my eyes facing Matt's room.

Kelly, a nurse who had worked with Matt previously and had met all my family, came over, her hands clasped in front of her.

"You should call your kids," she said softly. "Can I do that for you?"

I nodded numbly and handed her my phone after pulling up Nicole's contact info. Behind me I could still hear the beeps and shuffles of everyone in Matt's hospital room. Kelly came back minutes later and said Nicole had left right away to come to the hospital. She called my son, but it was early in Illinois, so he didn't answer. She gave me back the phone and said to let her know when he called.

"Can you call Matt's dad, too?" I whispered. There was no way I would be able to calmly talk to any of them to tell them what was happening. I had just put my phone away when Ryan called back, so I gave the phone to Kelly. Ryan was five hours away and so, even if he'd hopped in the car right away, he wouldn't have made it in time if...

I couldn't even let myself finish the thought. Ryan just needed to know what was happening. During this time, a nurse came out and said they'd got his airway back. Dr. Gray, who had tried to do the trach procedure the first time, had rushed from her office when she heard the code blue to check on Matt. She came over to me shortly afterward and just stood with me, her hand on my back, and told me that the trach was finally back in place.

"It was a lot," she said, "but things are where they need to be now. Your husband is tough."

"I know he is," I said, smiling through my tears.

When the accident happened that first night, I wasn't there and didn't know all that Matt went through. The thought that he'd felt all of that pain and was alone haunted me. The personal feelings that come over people when they're right there in the moment of a tragedy are immensely powerful. I will never again feel the same if I'm in a hospital and hear "code blue" again. I will stop whatever I'm doing and say a prayer for the person and their family as I know exactly what they're going through.

Once Matt was revived and stable again, the mass of people started to go back to their normal duties. Slowly, the chaos dissipated and finally Dr. Cox came out and explained all that had happened and what he'd done. The staff would need a few more minutes to reposition Matt and get him settled. Dr. Cox wanted me to know that, when I went back into Matt's room, he would not look the same. He explained that during the process, air had been pumped into Matt and so he was very bloated. His face would look really full. He was trying to prepare me for what I would see. I'm glad he did as I would not have reacted well to seeing Matt without this knowledge. He explained it would go down throughout the day.

While sitting waiting on the okay from Elanor to return to Matt's room, I checked my phone and realized I'd missed a text from Matt's sister. I'd forgotten to call her! I gathered all my strength and gave her a call to tell her what had just happened. I'm sure it was a lot for her to hear and she kept the phone call short.

I was allowed back into Matt's room and went right to him and said how sorry I was for not listening and not getting Elanor to get him back into bed. I felt guilty that if only I had been persistent and asked him to get back to bed sooner, maybe this might not have happened.

As the doctor warned, Matt's face was indeed very full, like he'd been pumped full of bee venom. I just sat next to him, touching his hand and waiting. I knew Nicole and Matt's parents were on their way. I talked to Ryan during that time, too, and told him that he should only come if he didn't have baseball he needed to get to. Ryan said he'd be able to leave in a couple of hours. It was comforting to me to know that both my kids would be there soon.

I watched Matt sleep for what must have been hours because, when I looked up, there was Nicole walking towards Matt's room. I went out in the hall and gave her a big hug. I don't think she understood how I was feeling after all that had happened that morning. I probably would not have had the same feeling if I had not been there going through it myself.

"Trust in the Lord with all your heart
and lean not on your own understanding;
in all your ways submit to him,
and he will make your paths straight."

(Prov 3:5-6) New International Version

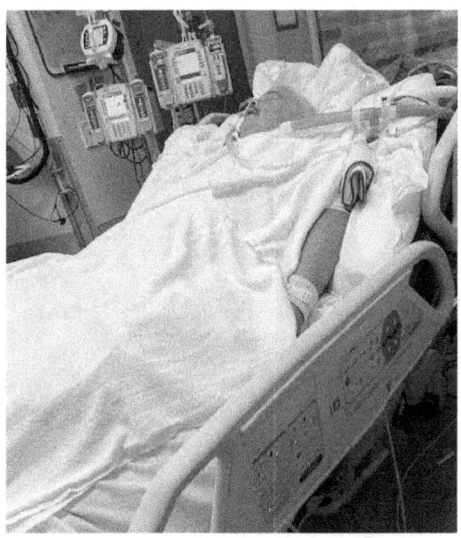

Picture of Matt after 18 days in
ICU and after coding.

DAY 19

During times in our lives when we are going through rough patches, the amount of support and generosity by those we love, acquaintances, and even complete strangers is very humbling. Nearly a month into Matt's recovery, I began to think about how to manage our money. It was easy to forget the practicalities and logistics of a hospital stay; as much as I'd love to believe that Matt was receiving all the care he needed without expectations from me, I knew that the bills would come due soon enough. We had money saved, and I had plenty of sick days so I could be off work and still get paid. I knew Matt had limited vacation days left and knew his pay would stop soon. I was also thinking about these hotel nights. I had tried really hard to find a close but reasonably cheap option for me. I asked the nurses about where to stay and got more information about a reasonable, safe hotel. I even investigated booking an Airbnb, and got a discount from a hotel in the hospital care program, but still the bill was going to add up. And with Matt's recovery moving forward in fits and starts, I also did not know how long to book. So, I did what I could to get the best rate, only booked for a few days at a time, and kept renewing. Without hesitation, I handed them my charge card and thought that I couldn't worry about that now.

That's when my family stepped in and I will always be grateful to them. Collectively, they told me that I wasn't going to have to worry about paying for hotel nights and they would get it figured out. I'd put it out of my mind at the beginning of all this, thinking I would circle around once Matt could go home and I could sit down with the paperwork. But when I went to check out of my first hotel, I found that the bill had been paid. Two different credit cards had paid for several nights, and my balance left was for only one night.

I was shocked. At least two of the nights I'd stayed in the hotel it was very expensive since I'd had a suite with Ryan and Nicole, but, beyond that, each night the bill had increased—and fast. To see that all but one night was paid in full was mind blowing. The kindness of whoever it was that went to the trouble of sending in their card information and paying for those nights was so overwhelming.

From the beginning of Matt's time in the ICU, God had provided what we needed. Family sent money to my son to help him pay for gas, since he had driven so far, and to help him out since I was very preoccupied and trying to manage everything myself. Each night when I left the hospital, all I could do was replay the previous few days. That was the beginning of the checks and money from coworkers, family, friends and complete strangers that would come in over the next few months to help us pay for all our expenses. I did not have to worry about money for gas, food, hotel, or any general necessities. It is amazing how God knows just what is needed and when.

One particular day, when I went home to check on the house and pets and do some things there to keep up, my daughter came over and brought me a card. Someone had gone to her-in-law's house and dropped off a gift and said they wanted to remain anonymous. I opened the card, which read *Just Because We Care.* Inside the card was $1,000. I started bawling. My heart was so full. Even though I had to watch my husband struggle, I felt uplifted because I knew God was in control and was by our side, especially when we needed it the most.

Weeks later, after Matt was recovered and we were home, I went back and added up all my hospital stay expenses. Through God and people who cared, I realized I had been given enough money to pay for all the nights in hotels during his forty-five days in the hospital. That allowed me to use my paychecks to continue to pay our bills. Through the generosity of others, one part of this ordeal at least was taken care of, leaving me without worry.

God works in mysterious ways. He has a plan for each and every one of us and he does not promise that we will never go through trials. What He does do is put situations in front of us to help build our love and compassion and to make us stronger people. This was definitely one of those times. I had days where I needed all the prayers I could get because my strength was low and needed work. I had days where I was a light for other people because I knew that God was taking care of us.

Prayers, not just from people I knew but complete strangers, and other followers of God, are what helped me to get through each day. A genuine connection with a higher power was present during those dark beginning days.

"And my God will meet all your needs according to the riches of his glory in Christ Jesus."

(Phil 4:19) New International Version

DAY 20

October 29, 2021, will always mean a lot to me. The impact of that day and all the extreme emotions that I had gone through while Matt was coding and hanging on for his life will never leave my thoughts. I replay it in my mind, even to this day, and I'm not sure how I made it through those minutes of pure torture.

However, I was quick to rebound because I knew I had to face my family and help them understand what happened. Thankfully, Matt had been resuscitated and slept calmly into the next day. My nerves, on the other hand, were still jangled and I had to remind myself often that he was still here and okay. Nicole, Ryan, and I spent some time together talking, but the biggest hurdle was reassuring my father in-law. He arrived at Matt's room first thing the next morning and just sat quietly with him for a while. We didn't say much to each other, but sat together and watched the calm rise and fall of Matt's chest. He was still puffy from the events of the code blue, but I could see some improvement. When we were walking out of the room to meet up with the rest of the family, I remember my father-in-law looking down at his son, his eyes filled with sadness. I put my arm around his shoulder as we slowly walked past the other rooms and nurses' station and said,

"It's going to be okay."

"If you say so," he replied.

"He's still here." I rubbed his shoulder.

Later that day, I got a video from the teacher in my classroom. It was so good to see the kids after such a stressful day; I don't know if they'll ever appreciate what a gift it was to see something so joyful and...normal. I was almost jealous that I wasn't there and that I was missing the day with them. But as any teacher knows, the days near Halloween in an elementary classroom are some of the toughest. As much as I felt I was facing a battle each day for Matt's survival, I know that my coworkers and substitute teacher were in the trenches in their own way.

During those days when things were extremely hard, I relished the insignificant things like quiet times in Matt's room or dinner time with family. Who knew that a simple meal of orange chicken and rice could mean so much? Even though many times I was so distracted when I ate that I didn't even really taste it, going through the motions of eating, because I knew I'd needed it, the comfort of a simple meal, was still a good one.

Sunday was Halloween. It wasn't a big celebratory holiday for us since our children were grown, but it was still a sweet thing to see the hospital decked out in fun holiday decorations. That day, Matt was awake and turned towards the window when I got there. Beth, his nurse that day, had drawn Halloween designs on the lidocaine patches on his chest to be festive. Even though these patches had been on his chest since the surgery to help alleviate pain, this was the first time I'd truly noticed them. I laughed, taking in the detail of the drawings: a ghost, witch, and a pumpkin. This, among many other instances, reminded me that my husband was well-cared for. Even though we had been through a very near-death experience two days before, Beth knew how to lighten the mood.

Matt dozed for a while but eventually woke up. I always liked those times the best, obviously, because with each passing day, Matt was becoming more and more himself. The progress was still slow, but he was getting there. However, it was also extremely hard because he was always asking to leave or get out of bed and that was not happening. He hated being restrained but it was necessary with the way he would act when he was awake. When he was awake, he would get so agitated and have a challenging time being still. He was still very fragile, especially after coding the other day and having to go through chest compressions only two weeks post-surgery. He had been through so much and he would wear himself out.

However, on Halloween, he asked me to get him out of bed.

I shook my head and said, "I'm not strong enough to do that."

Without missing a beat, he pointed to Ryan and mouthed "He is."

Ryan looked his dad straight in the eye and told him he couldn't do that. Matt asked why not, and Ryan explained that he would get in trouble. Matt sank back down into the bed with the biggest look of defeat. His eyes closed and his head relaxed, and he slowly went back to sleep, so Ryan and I took Beth's advice and headed "out" for lunch. No cafeteria food. She'd given us an address of a unique food court market she thought we would like.

"You need to take some time for yourself while he's sleeping," she'd said. We did just that. It was freeing to eat somewhere outside of the hospital during the daylight. It was a gorgeous day, and the fresh outside air felt so good. Some of the best medicine. After Ryan and I had lunch, he left to go back to school, and I took some time to clean out my car. I had so much in there since I had been living out of it and my hotel.

That was the day the doctors and nurses started talking about moving Matt to a long-term care facility. I was so unsure about what it was like or what his care would be there and did not really like the unknown. I had gotten comfortable with the staff in the ICU; however, I wanted him better so that was the next step. They were trying to get him breathing better and off drugs through an IV before they would move him. The problem was *Matt*. He would be fine for a few days and then *bam*, something would happen that wouldn't enable him to be moved. Once, there was fluid in his lungs, so they had to drain that. Another time, he ran a fever.

I remembered at the beginning of his ICU stay a case manager talked to me about the progression of care. They projected that Matt would stay a few weeks in the ICU, then a long-term care facility, then in patient rehab, then at home rehab, with the entire process possibly taking months. A big wave of emotions swept over me at that time as I realized the scope of time we were looking at until Matt was "back to normal."

To make matters worse, during 2021, the world was still coping with Covid restrictions. I had told my job that I'd probably be out a few weeks, and Matt only had a few weeks of vacation saved up—but now we were looking at *months* before he'd be able to return home without care or treatment. And that was *if* there were no other major setbacks.

The hospital looked for places for him in Illinois so we could be closer to home, but the only places available that would be covered by insurance were just as far away as we were in the ICU.

The last time Matt had been in a car accident, we'd been home in a matter of days. But now, with such a great stretch of time in front of us, it felt like we'd never get home again. As much as I know Matt was frustrated, restless, and bored—so was I. Most of the time he was sleeping, which he needed to do, of course, but that left me in the silence of the hospital room with little TV, papers to grade, or maybe Nicole and I watching Netflix. There's only so much television a person can watch! I'd quickly get tired of sitting, but didn't want to stand and risk waking Matt. I longed to walk around the hospital but was terrified of missing something.

Living a life where I had no control was not a good feeling. Other people made all the decisions for me. So, I hung onto what I could control: texting updates to people, showing up every day, tasks for work, and my prayers.

"Jesus looked at them and said, "With man this is impossible, but with God all things are possible."

(Matt 19:26) New International Version

DAY 21

October rolled into November. Matt had been in the hospital for twenty-one days. It felt like an eternity, but had only been three weeks. However, all the days had some significance in my life. I never knew what I might find on any given day. Was this the day they'd move him? Was he going to get up again? Would he be open to talk? Also, the doctors worried about delirium setting in since he'd been here awhile and had been on some strong medicine for his pain and agitation. I learned so many new drug names.

Ketamine.

Fentanyl.

Propofol.

The idea that Matt's body was full of these drugs did worry me, though there was no way he could have handled his recovery without them. I thought constantly about the adverse effects the drugs could have on him, how they could affect his memory or his cognition. Some days, he would appear calm but it never seemed to last and so they would give him more drugs. Some days, I felt like I was on a roller coaster. There's always the long struggle to climb the hill and then the thrill of plunging down the other side, at times turning upside down and then arriving back at the station with a screeching halt. That's the fun part—because then, as you're out of breath and excited, you get let out of your seat and have the time and the space to calm down.

Going through this constant roller coaster afforded me no time to calm down or process the adrenaline of Matt's ups and downs. I was stuck and the roller coaster would go again. That was what it was like for that whole first week of November. Matt would have a fantastic day, and then a day where he was so agitated nothing could settle him. Then calm again. It was like he was there but not there. I longed for the days of normal, but we just could not get him well enough to leave the ICU and move to the next steps.

During this time, my work put me on FMLA leave because I'd missed so many days. After the social worker got my paperwork filled out and sent it to my employer, she gave me a copy. My heart dropped and I went into shock when I read that I was approved to be gone for a year.

I thought for sure Matt and I would be home long before a year was up, but here was confirmation in my hands that he was going to have a longer road ahead than we'd thought, complete with the apprehension of long-term disability. I remember the sinking feeling of dread at the thought I would have to be the sole provider for the family. This was just too much.

All I could do was pray. Prayers for God to help Matt heal and get us home and on with our lives. Prayers for him to be okay and able to do things. My always-on-the-go husband did not deserve to be held back on his pursuits in life; the thought of him not being able to weld or fly or work in his shop was devastating. *Deep breath,* I thought, *and pray and wake up each day looking and working toward progress.* God had to have a plan for us. I knew He would take care of us but wasn't sure where this was going.

As the week went on, we moved into day 22… then day 23 of

recovery… and Matt began to act differently again. The roller coaster kept going. We went through more tests to figure out what was going on. Test in the morning, wait all day for a result, wait to hear from the doctor who would come up with a plan. I learned very quickly that while we were waiting for results, it was always helpful to ask the nurses for updates. They know everything going on in the hospital and so talking to them helped me feel better when the waits got long.

I would spend my days talking with the nurses, not only about Matt but also about our lives. Beth was often Matt's nurse and she and I had really gotten to having general life conversations. While waiting for results one day, Beth and I talked about the best books for second graders. Her son was in second grade and that was also what I was teaching at the time. My mind drew an absolute blank on titles since I'd been away from my normal routine for so long, so I texted a friend and asked for her recommendations. Some, Beth's son had already read, but a few were new options she wanted to get for her son. It was those days and conversations that helped take me away from the long stretches sitting by Matt's bedside. The nurses, women like Beth, made me feel like I had friends.

It wasn't long before it was discovered that Matt had fluid in or around his lungs again. He was sent down for a procedure to start the line to drain them. Matt did what he always did when any new procedure was attempted; he was not calm, and his oxygen dropped.

They were going to have to figure out another way. After many discussions, it was decided to call in a thoracic consultant. I couldn't understand why they couldn't do the procedure like before; they'd put chest tubes in once and removed them, so I thought it should be easy to repeat the process. But that wasn't their plan. Since Matt had been having so much agitation and uneasiness, they wanted another opinion.

When the thoracic consultant came in, Matt was sedated and seemed calm enough since the meds had just been administered.

The consultant said, "We're doing this bedside."

I tried to explain that Matt didn't respond well to procedures. The thoracic consultant shook his head. "This is a simple process and he appears to be fine right now." I couldn't help but feel nervous when I noticed that he didn't seem to know much about Matt's history and didn't take my concerns into account.

"What drugs does he take at home?" he asked.

"None."

"He must be taking something since he seems to respond well here."

I repeated my answer: Matt did not take any medications at home. I tried not to feel offended at the implication laced in the doctor's tone. I turned and glanced at Nicole, looking at her face for confirmation of what I thought I was hearing. Not just prescription drugs, but illegal ones. He was asking if my husband was an addict.

The doctor continued saying that they would plan on the bedside procedure tomorrow, trying to placate me by assuring me they would also have anesthesia in the room if that was necessary. I reluctantly agreed, though strongly suggested that this was not the best for Matt.

I felt very confused and uneasy about this situation. I mean, he was implying that Matt was on drugs since he appeared to be handling them so well. But he was not, and they didn't last long, and each time he woke up he grew more and more anxious and agitated. Maybe the drugs he was being given in the hospital were doing the opposite and really having a strange effect on him.

To try and put me at ease, the thoracic consultant asked the anesthesiologist to talk to me. When he arrived, though, I was not at all comforted.

"I don't know why he asked me to be here, quite frankly," the anesthesiologist said, "Your husband looks okay, but I can't really do anything here in the room if needed."

"He looks okay now," I said, "But he gets really overworked when anything like this happens. I'm worried something like that will happen again."

The anesthesiologist was concerned and asked permission to do a test to see how awake and aware Matt was, even though he looked calm and relaxed. I said "Please do." He came back a little later and attached leads to Matt's head and collected some data. Matt performed well, which proved my point that he was more awake and could realize what was happening.

"Wow," the anesthesiologist remarked. "This is definitely unusual. When we perform a procedure, you need patients to be at a certain level of 'out of it.' Your husband has been given the normal dose of anesthesia but doesn't reach that level we're looking for. This means that he's likely aware, on some level, of the procedures being done, which is obviously not good."

My heart sank, as I thought of all the things Matt had gone through that he was likely aware of—that he *felt*. No wonder he sent himself into a panic spiral every time a doctor tried to repeat the procedures.

The anesthesiologist said he did not have any say so, but would report his findings to the doctor. A while later, the doctor came back and agreed to take Matt to the operating room to put the tubes in. It would be a short and easy procedure, but the best thing was for Matt to be put completely under. I felt vindicated, though also aware that any time Matt underwent anesthesia there was increased risk of complications, too.

After this whole back and forth, I reflected on my frustration with the doctor. I'd texted my family, too, and kept them abreast of everything that was happening.

Do I need to come kick some ass? my brother texted.

No, I responded, *I did it myself.*

Though I didn't have much patience for the thoracic specialist, I was proud of myself for standing up for Matt, challenging the assertion that my husband had to be on drugs, and pushing to find the real solution instead of letting supposition and assumptions stand. I knew in my heart what was right and refused to stand for anything less. I remember being livid and thinking "How dare that doctor accuse us of that?" But then I reflected that, to him, we were just another pair of breathing human beings—patients in a room that would be filled with other patients soon enough. We meant absolutely nothing to him. He didn't understand our situation.

Sympathy crept in, despite my anger. What was the best action? Pray for him. He was good at what he did, even though he had no personality or bedside manner when it came to his patients.

"But I tell you, love your enemies
and pray for those who persecute you."

(Matt 5:44) New International Version

DAY 25

I'd been driving to the store the previous day when the thoracic specialist called me to say the tubes would be put in the next morning—a Friday—in the operating room and that if I wanted to see Matt before we went in, I should be to the hospital by 7:30 a.m. I thanked him and assured him I'd be there. I spent that evening relaxing and trying to get to sleep early in order to wake up early to get to the hospital.

That next morning—day 25—the alarm sounded, jolting me out of a rare deep sleep. I got up, showered to refresh myself, and prepared to face this doctor again. When I got to the hospital, I was stopped at the front desk and told it wasn't yet visiting hours.

"My husband is having surgery this morning," I insisted.

"No surgeries are done this early," was the reply.

I felt my anger rising again. "My husband is in the ICU and they're taking him down soon. You have to let me by."

They finally relented, but when I got to Matt's room I was met with flustered and angry nurses. "The transport has already tried to take him down, but since you weren't here to sign the consent forms, we couldn't move him."

Apparently, they'd already tried to move Matt down to surgery before I arrived, so we were quickly escorted to an elevator down to the surgery wing. Once off the elevator, we stopped in a line of other patients waiting for an open operating room. Suddenly, our surgeon came down the hallway in a huff, shaking papers in front of him. He was furious because there wasn't a signed consent.

"I don't understand?" I asked.

"You signed it for a bedside procedure, which is what we were originally going to do today," he explained. However, when the surgeon looked at Matt's medical records, the consent wasn't there. It had been removed by someone else since we'd adjusted the plan and it wasn't going to happen bedside anymore. Unbeknown to me, a new consent form was required for the operating room. The surgeon told his assistant to get my signature. I hurriedly signed the forms there in the hallway, and they were whisked away to be processed and filed. Our surgeon left in a huff. I'm not sure where he was going as the surgery was supposed to happen soon.

Finally, Matt was wheeled back and I retreated to the waiting room to again count the minutes until I had an update. Not long after, I was notified that Matt was out and all was good. The nurses and doctors of the ICU were true advocates for their patients. They certainly took care of Matt and looked out for what was best for him. If it hadn't been for the nurses in the ICU holding Matt and waiting for the correct consent form, I can only imagine what would have happened. I still think of the anesthesiologist, too, the man who was thoughtful and inquisitive enough to explore all avenues for Matt and who finally determined the root cause of his extreme anxiety. Their combined efforts once again saved Matt's life. The staff that week hold a special place in my heart for their work in finding out what was wrong with Matt and doing what they thought was best.

"In you, Lord my God,
I put my trust.
[2] I trust in you;
do not let me be put to shame,
nor let my enemies triumph over me."

(Ps 25:1-2) New International Version

DAY 25

After the procedure—500-600 ccs of fluid drained from Matt's chest—he rested much more peacefully, his breathing smoothed and even. I decided to check in with work and was given permission to go to school after the students had left for the day. It was surreal to walk into school after being gone for a little over three weeks, like visiting a house you used to live in, but which has since been redecorated by new owners. Everything was where I remembered, but subtle changes in the school made my absence feel more acute. The bulletin boards had changed for the seasons, minor things around the hallways had been rearranged or removed. I hadn't ever been one to miss a lot of days, so it was even more surreal to know that I'd be missing even more than I already had.

When I walked into my classroom, I just stood in the doorway taking in the scene. There were papers in huge piles on my desk, there were pencils laying around the room—all of them unsharpened—and my usually neat and organized desk groupings were misshapen and misaligned. Nothing too serious, so I got to work to fix it to my liking. While I worked some teachers were still in the building and saw me. They were cautious but happy to see me and gave me big hugs and talked to me for a bit. The outpouring of love and support was huge. Tears formed in my eyes just talking to them. Wanting to get things done and cleaned up to be able to meet up with my mom and my sister, I politely excused myself.

I quickly got to work and reorganized my desks, sharpened pencils, and got out new ones to replenish student pencils. I went through piles of papers, sorting ones I looked at, and putting Post-it notes and directions on top of other piles. By the time I left, the room was not too bad. I could have easily spent several hours doing so many things to help the person who had taken over for me. However, I was on leave and was just trying to help. My time home was limited, and I had plans later with my mom and sister.

I remember feeling a bit jealous as I drove home; my sister was on her way to visit our dad who was in a nursing home and currently hopping in and out of doctor's offices with various ailments. I missed him, but because of Covid-19 and Matt's condition, I couldn't risk spreading anything. I was careful who I was around and kept myself well to be with him every day. So, I just told my sister to give our dad a hug and kiss from me and tell him that I missed him. She promised she would, but the pang of sadness I felt that I couldn't do it myself was still there.

When I got home, I did my best to stay busy with little activities—laundry, straightening, clearing out the refrigerator—until my mom and sister were at my house with a pizza for dinner. I hugged them both, leaning into their hugs and crying with them. This was the first time I'd seen my mom in person since Matt's accident. She was my rock, even from a distance, but to have her holding me here was a balm I hadn't known I needed. Seeing her on this day, a little over three weeks after the accident, allowed me to let my guard down and let the tears flow out.

We sat in my living room, eating pizza and just talking. I was updated about Dad, and we had some good girl time. My mom had not been able to leave him to see me. She was dealing with his care while I was handling Matt's. I left all the decisions and help up to my siblings since I was not able to handle or be in two places at the same time. When they left, I finished laundry and cleaned up and then settled in to sleep in my own bed.

The bed was very lonely, and I just stared at Matt's empty spot. I slept closer to the middle, trying to feel his presence next to me.

"Therefore encourage one another and build each other up, just as in fact you are doing."

(1 Thess. 5:11) New International Version

DAYS 26 – 29

The next morning, I got up and ready, made sure everything at home was locked up tight, and got on the road back to Indianapolis. I was exhausted, despite having slept through the night. My eyes felt heavy and scratchy like sandpaper, my joints sore from all the hours spent in hospital chairs, my back tight from leaning over to hold Matt's hand. Hospital stays—whether you're the patient or the family—are not for the weak. I wished I could snap my fingers and be there.

When I pulled into the dark parking garage, I made my way to the second level to find a spot close to the elevator and stairwell. I usually left the hospital at night and wanted to make sure I'd be near a light. The parking garage noises at night were strange and people could sneak up on you without knowing. The less I had to walk the better, when I was by myself.

As I entered Matt's room, the nurse, Renee, was taking out the staples from his chest. I asked her to count them for me, so she did.

"1, 2, 3," she began. Soon she was at 15, 16, 17, 18 … 22, 23 … 35, 36 … 48, 49. She had taken out forty-nine staples from his left side chest all the way to the right side of his back, under his arm. Then a little later, she wanted to move his blood pressure cuff and realized there were two more staples on a cut on his left arm.

This was an uneventful day, though having his staples removed was a wonderful step in the right direction. I just sat with Matt. He was awake some. I talked with him about what he'd been through, but little did I know that he wouldn't remember anything of the past twenty-six days. He rested. I sat. He'd wake up and ask for things. I'd try to help, then he'd sleep some more, and I'd sit. I did my best to check papers, read emails, enter assignments online for my students and watch videos on my phone. And the pattern continued.

Lately, Nicole was staying home more and only coming over to be with me a few days a week—most weeks, she stayed with me from Tuesday to Thursday and then went home for four days. Ryan was busy with classes and couldn't come over as often since school was so far away. He would call and text often to check on his dad. Weirdly, when I was on my own, I'd often wish for someone else there to talk to. But on the occasion that someone would visit—a nurse, a friend, or even a family member—I'd find myself wanting to be alone again, as the effort of maintaining conversations was just too draining. How could I be so fickle? I wanted company but I dreaded having to answer everyone's questions when they were there. Only two people could be in the room at a time, so when people come to visit, I had to leave the room and go up to the fifth floor waiting room. We'd sit and talk and then usually go to the cafeteria. I was getting tired of the cafeteria. The food was on rotation, and I'd been there long enough to try anything I wanted. Also, the cafeteria was either busy and had a lot of food selections or empty and little to choose from. The biggest reprieve was being able to take my mask off; I know the precautions existed for a very good reason, but being in a mask nearly all day every day was really wearing on me. I had a new appreciation for the doctors and nurses who'd had to do that their entire careers.

The next few days were all the same and I just showed up every day to be with Matt. He was doing well, and the doctors were still weaning him off the medicines so he could eventually transfer to a long-term care facility. I posted updates on Facebook for our friends, family, and others praying for Matt. I ended each post with "each day is a new day on the road to recovery." I'm not sure if I believed it or not, but I was trying to be positive, despite knowing that the road ahead of us was still quite long and full of obstacles we hadn't anticipated yet. I wasn't sure if the end would ever be in sight and felt like each day was the same—except for those moments when things went absolutely haywire.

In my head, I'd cycled back to the very beginning of this ordeal where it felt like Matt wasn't making any progress at all. The changes were so minute, that I worried we'd be in the hospital forever. I'd seen the room next to Matt's be a revolving door for patients. There was a new person there every day or two; meanwhile, he and I occupied the same room day in and day out. When was it going to be Matt's turn? When would I get to feel like we were making a change, and Matt would breathe on his own and not need medicine to keep him calm?

Little by little, though, encouraging changes started to happen. The plans were to lower and eventually stop Matt's IV medicines and have him complete his breathing trials. He was breathing. He was getting his meds lowered. A little each day. I answered his same questions. Although it felt very redundant, having some normalcy and consistency had to be good, right?

DAY 30

The morning of Matt's thirtieth day in the ICU began just like a usual weekday, with Nicole and I getting up, getting ready, eating some breakfast, grabbing coffee, and going to the hospital. As we walked into Matt's room, I immediately noticed something different. Matt was wearing some type of gown—it was heavier than his normal hospital gown and oddly colorful in such a sterile room. Normally, he was hot a lot of the time and never wanted a gown on. When I greeted him that morning, he acted differently. He didn't acknowledge me, wouldn't look my way, and did not try to talk. The nurse tried to prompt him by saying, "Look who's here!" in her best sing-song voice. Matt just rolled his eyes and looked away.

Confused, I looked to the nurse for answers, but her forehead was furrowed in concentration and concern. This was not Matt. I tried talking to him and pointing out Nicole. All we got was blank stares.

Delirium, we finally concluded. Talking to the nurses afterward, I learned that it's often associated with confusion, disorientation, and even hallucinations. They thought that he'd been on heavy drugs for so long that he was too confused. He didn't know who Nicole and I were. I was not at all prepared for the emotional toll that day; up until then, Matt had always been awake or recognized me when I came into the room. No matter what pain he was in, he knew who I was and that I was here for him, but today his eyes were unfocused; he was very distant and non-responsive to anything I asked. The nurse asked me if I knew if anything happened overnight, but I didn't, as I would have had to call before the shift change at 7:00 a.m.

We found out later that the night had not been a good one for Matt. He had been on so many strong medicines for a long time, and it finally caught up to him. He was going through delirium. He had become confused and disoriented. He was not able to think or remember. During the night, he was in such a state that he did not respond to anything with the nurse. They took him down to CT to find out what was wrong. For weeks they'd been trying to slowly wean him off the IV medicines like ketamine but the night before, with the onset of his delirium, they'd quit all of the drugs cold turkey!

So, by the time I arrived in the morning, and he'd not had any drugs for several hours and was going through withdrawal. I tried to calculate: for the past month, Matt's body had been pumped full of heavy drugs every day just to relieve pain, sedate him, and keep his anxiety at bay. One whole month of drugs I knew some people become addicted to for life. I couldn't begin to imagine the horrible withdrawal he would feel.

I tried showing him pictures from my phone. A big blank stare was all I got. Then the noise began—weird grunts and burping sounds. Then his eyes rolled back into his head, his gaze unfocused, his skin sheened with sweat. Nervous, I talked with Kelly, the nurse, and consoled Nicole who was distraught to see her father this way, too. The nurse assured us that Matt was going to be closely monitored, but that it would take time for the drugs to leave his system and for him to settle into a more restful state. She advised us that it could get ugly and that, if we wanted to step away for a while, they would keep us posted.

We got in our car and drove to a mall. It was cool, damp, and cloudy but the outlook outside was better than what we'd faced inside. We spent a few hours walking through the mall, trying on clothes and shoes. Anything to take our mind off the worries and struggles from the past month and especially from that morning. While sitting eating lunch, my mind kept going back to Matt. I didn't want to talk about it to Nicole since this morning had really upset her. Watching the people and the hustle and bustle of daily life reminded me that this was not where we were. Our life had revolved around one thing, and shopping and working were not a part of our picture.

We went back to the hospital later that afternoon. Not much had changed in Matt's behavior. I stayed with him for a while, but checked out early and called it a night. That night, I prayed so hard that the next day would be better. Not having Matt at home was hard, but seeing him like that—a shell of the person I love—was the hardest pill I've ever had to swallow.

The next day, Matt was a little better. We were able to check in on him briefly before Nicole went home to see Collin and a few hours after that I drove home, too. That afternoon, they'd done a test on Matt's bronchial tubes, and I waited for the results before I left which put me home later.

The next morning, I woke up and dawdled getting ready to head back to Indianapolis. I felt guilty for not being on the road, so I called in and checked on Matt. Alex, Matt's nurse for the day, said he was having a good morning. He told me there was no rush—that I could take my time and relax. I listened and spent more time doing things around the house. After a bit I decided to leave anyway to get there because after him not knowing me just a few days ago, I wanted to be there to talk if he was alert and doing better.

After my long tedious drive, I walked into Matt's room and Alex said, "I thought you were going to stay home today."

I said, "Well I stayed later but just cannot stay away. This is where I want to be."

That afternoon, after a wonderful morning, Matt started to change again. He grew agitated and fickle. Even the doctor came in and said, "I wish you could have seen him this morning." Talk about a stab through my heart, and I instantly regretted taking extra time for myself that morning. I know that wasn't the doctor's intention but, after having so many days of bad, to miss this one glimmer of good made me feel awash with guilt.

So, as I sat there that afternoon, trying to help ease Matt's discomfort, I kept saying "This is where I need to be." It was frustrating however, because he just could not get comfortable. After Alex spent time taking care of Matt and I took a break, Matt began to calm down and they gave him a bath and a shave. They said he had to look good for me and we were going to get a date night! The nurses all acted and helped to spiff up Matt, brought in a light that changed color, and arranged the bed and chairs so that I could be closer. They even turned down the lights to create a soft, romantic ambience. I was really touched at their thoughtfulness and, even if Matt didn't or couldn't express it, I think he was, too.

The nurses even shut his door, which, I realized, was the first time that had happened the whole time we'd been there. They drew the curtains and turned on the TV, flipping through the channels until they found a movie for us. So, there we were, on our first date night after Matt's accident, holding hands in the dim light of the hospital room. It was a night I will never forget.

It was also on that night I took a picture of us and sent it to people for them to be able to see him. He'd been in such terrible shape before that I hadn't documented any of it that way, but here we were, almost feeling like normal. My post received a lot of feedback from friends and family, between my page and Nicole's page. In the picture, Matt is smiling and looking directly at the camera, the most alert and attentive I'd seen him in several days. Many of the comments from friends and family reflected on our smiles. Their words warmed my heart.

Words like: *"Hang in there, Matt!"*

"Have a wonderful date night."

"That's the best news all day!!"

"Love the smiles."

"Love nurses who go above and beyond!"

"Wow, seeing both of your faces is great."

"It is so nice to see the smiles!"

"Praise God!"

"How wonderful!!"

We had such a good evening. I stayed longer than usual and we enjoyed our time together. Matt's sister and brother-in-law were coming the next day, and I texted them when I left for the evening, telling them if he were acting this way tomorrow, they would have a great visit.

"Praise be to the God and Father of our Lord Jesus Christ,
the Father of compassion and the God of all comfort,
who comforts us in all our troubles,
so that we can comfort those in any trouble with the comfort
we ourselves receive from God."

(1 Corinthians 1:3-4) New International Version

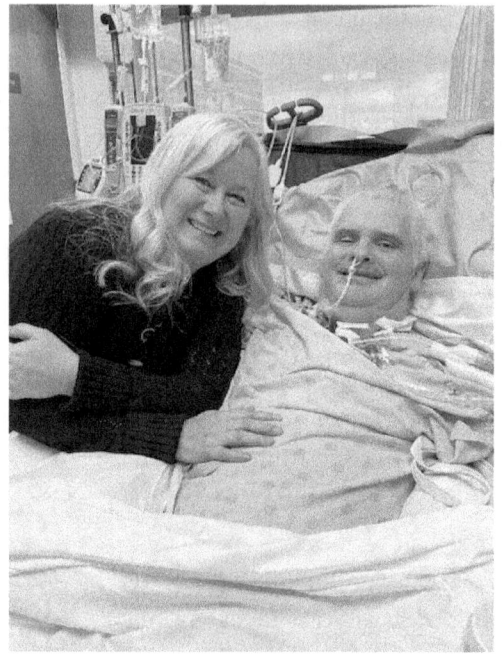

The nurses set up our room for us to have a date night.

DAY 33

As I walked to my car at the hotel that wonderful Sunday morning, after the memorable date night with Matt, I was feeling hopeful and good about how things were beginning to change and go well. I felt today was going to be a good day. After thirty-three days of ups and downs, it seemed like we were finally on a true upward trajectory. To top it off, it was beginning to snow. Beautiful snowflakes drifted over my car and fell in my hair me as I walked to the car. Even though I was a little cold, since I hadn't brought a jacket over from home yet (keeping an eye on the weather was always Matt's thing), I didn't mind.

I arrived and parked as usual and headed up to the fourth floor to see my date from last night. His bed had been turned, and was facing the window so Matt could watch the snow. I went and stood by him, and he greeted me with a smile. We stayed that way, watching the snow for some time, until the doctor came by for his rounds. His words were encouraging, and he liked Matt being able to see outside. Being cooped up in this room for so long could be hard on a person but having a chance to look out was good for healing. We continued to just sit and relax and wait for Matt's sister.

The weather made the trip longer than usual for Matt's family, but they made it. When they arrived, there were hugs all around when I met them in the lobby and they went in to see Matt while I waited in the waiting area, per the guidelines. Matt was awake and wanted to write down what he wanted to say. Up until that time—and even somewhat now—Matt's hands had been so swollen he wasn't able to even grip a pen. But now that he was truly awake and off most medicines, the swelling was beginning to come down. As I walked Matt's family out for them to head home, my brother-in-law handed me a dry erase board he'd gotten in the gift shop. After being in Matt's room earlier, he felt Matt needed it. I was thankful but remarked that writing was difficult. He thought he noticed Matt was trying to signal to write.

After they left, I went back to Matt's room and talked to him about the day. He motioned for the board. I gave it to him to write. Even though I could tell Matt was trying so hard to write letters and tell me something, all I got were scribbles. I took a picture and sent it to my sister-in-law and told her to ask her husband what it said. He responded quickly.

It clearly says, 'I have the best brother-in-law ever.'

To this day, this is one of our best memories and we chuckle every time.

Even though it was a weekend, the doctors began to *finally* process Matt's move. He was improving and medically stable and ready. I could have wept with relief knowing that he was, at last, ready to move forward. One more step toward home. One more step toward my family back in one piece.

> *"Trust in the LORD with all your heart*
> *and lean not on your own understanding."*
>
> *(Prov 3:5) New International Version*

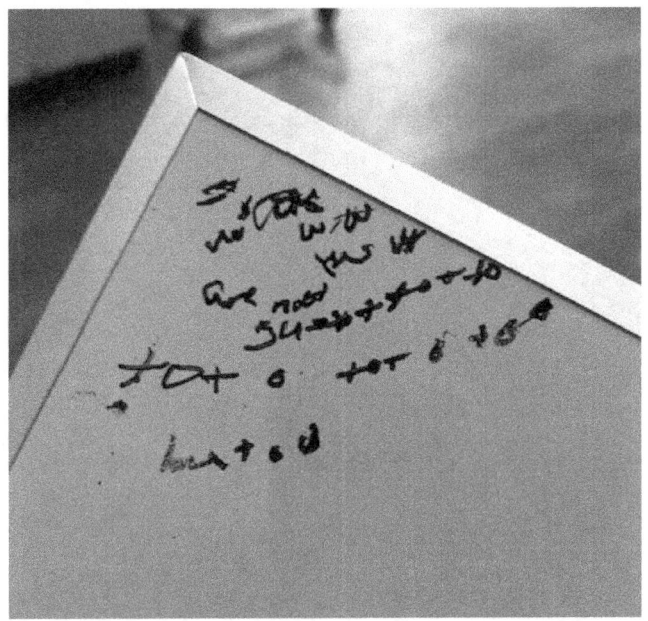

Matt's brother-in-law bought Matt a dry erase board because he thought he needed to write to tell us what he wants. This is what Matt was able to write.

DAY 38

Remember I said weekend? Yes, well what doctors want and what insurance (and people who only work through the week when they feel like it!) are two different things. We waited for insurance approval for four days and still had not heard anything. According to the doctors, Matt no longer needed to be in the ICU. He wasn't critical nor needed critical care anymore. I reminded myself to trust that there is a greater purpose behind life's events. That day, the doctors informed us they would move Matt down to the progressive care unit until there was word from the long-term care facility. We would just have to wait until a bed became available. The past four days had been long as Matt was awake, much more coherent, and wanted things, but was frustrated not to be able to get them for himself yet. However, he was able to write on his board and also able to use his phone himself.

It seemed that the closer Matt got to any sort of movement away from the ICU, the busier his room got. There were hospital staff in and out most of the day, running tests, checking on him, and preparing other things in the room to help him move along. It made it hard for me to step away for any kind of meal or break. I didn't want to miss anyone coming in who might have an update.

The most miraculous thing on the thirty-eighth day, was that Matt got his voice back! He'd been given a cap to put over his trach opening which would allow him to be heard when he tried to speak. After a month, my husband's voice met my ears again. To say that it was emotional was an understatement. It was like hearing his voice for the first time. I promised myself that I would never take it for granted that he could say my name, or that I could call for him and he'd answer.

Also that day, the hospital sent a therapist to do a swallow test to see how Matt's esophagus was after being ventilated and on a trach for so long. Many preparations were made to begin rehab until there was a change in floors or hospitals. Even though Matt was still hooked up to the ventilator, they had decided not to have any airflow through it. He had officially been without ventilator help for twenty-four hours, and the swallow tests proved to be good, so Matt could get liquids. His first food by mouth since October 11, thirty-eight days ago. He started slowly, with thickened soup and something to drink. They kept the feeding tube in to continue nutrition for the time being. He would need the strength for physical therapy.

Nicole and I spent a long time that day waiting for Matt to get moved but it did not happen while we were there. I had seen other patients leave and wanted Matt to have the same goodbye as others, and I really wanted to be there when it happened. But visiting hours ended that evening with no transfer in sight so I kissed him on the cheek and promised I'd be back first thing in the morning. However, at almost ten that night, Matt sent me a text telling me his new room number and that he was being moved. No one from the hospital bothered to let me know about Matt moving. I only knew because he told me.

I was very elated and could not wait for the morning to get

back and see Matt in his new room. It was hard to sleep with all the thankful emotions going through my head. My alarm was set for an early wakeup call the next day to be there first thing.

I walked into unfamiliar territory that morning—a new hospital floor, new people, and a new room setup. But Matt was beaming, thrilled to have this huge marker of progress, and we grinned at each other. He told me they'd packed up any possessions from his previous room and brought them to the new room and they were over in the closet across from his bed. It was strange, but Matt almost seemed sad to leave his old room. The surgical trauma critical care floor, and more specifically room 4212, had been Matt's home for thirty-eight days. We both had grown remarkably close with the nursing staff and felt comfortable with them. It was bittersweet to realize that we might never see those men and women again. But we definitely weren't sad enough to want to go back!

Matt began telling me about last night and that they packed things up and got his bed ready to roll. The pushed him straight out his room, past other rooms, and past the nurse's station. Since he had been there so long, everyone knew who he was and, at his exit, they lined up in the hall and clapped for him. It was like a parade. Matt waved as he passed the line of nurses and staff. They were happy for him to be promoted out of the ICU.

After hearing his story, I went through his things. The soft light we'd used on date night was there and so was a card the nurses used for Matt to communicate with them. I knew they didn't belong to us, so Nicole and I took them back to the fourth floor. When I walked to the nurses' station, Beth said "He got moved and isn't here."

I said, "Yes but these things belong here and aren't his." I also expressed to them that no one told me about his move but him.

The day nurses have a better connection with the families since they're there at the same time and naturally let the family know more about what goes on with the patients. I think at night they know the family isn't there and are sleeping, so informing the family isn't a priority.

The hospital was still waiting to hear from insurance about moving Matt to a different facility but began working with him on physical therapy. I know Matt was excited to move again, but because of the challenges he faced while in the ICU, his bed was equipped with an alarm if he got up, so even trying to reposition himself could set it off. Now that he was feeling so much better and moving, the alarm became a nuisance, but I know they were just protecting themselves and Matt.

There were plans to work on removing the feeding tube and also the trach. Matt was talking and getting along great while resting and healing and even doing all his own breathing and eating what food he could. Who knows why the insurance wasn't responding, but after meeting with the doctor who saw notes from the physiotherapist, they changed their recommendation from long term care to inpatient rehab which could be done in Champaign.

HOME!

I would be able to live at home and just visit Matt during the day with a short 25-minute drive! I was so excited. This sudden change in treatment plan sparked a whirlwind as we tried to talk to a case manager and made calls to the hospital for acceptance and insurance, but things were truly rolling for the good. The day had been remarkably busy but full of good news, but because it was Friday, even though everything had been set into motion, we'd likely have to wait over the weekend.

That same day, though, I got a call from the Long-Term Care

facility telling me they were expecting Matt. After hearing the purpose for the call, I was surprised and confused since it had been proposed for Matt's care to go home and he wasn't supposed to be going there anymore.

"You should call someone," I told the bewildered person on the other end of the line. "Things have changed, and I don't think Matt's going to long term care anymore."

The man on the phone thanked me for the update and said he would make the necessary changes. Notifications must have gotten delayed which allowed more time to skip this step-in recovery, but also did not relay that information to everyone involved. Moving there could have added a week to Matt's stay, as they would have wanted time to evaluate and monitor him. Thanksgiving was next week, and so no major decisions would be made about a release for the holiday. I decided to go home that weekend since I knew things were not changing on the weekend days. I traveled back to Indy by myself but began making plans for Thanksgiving with the family in a hotel in Indianapolis since we had not heard any news yet.

During these few days in the Progressive Care Unit, Matt was making improvements and they removed the feeding tube and the trach. One morning when I was not there, Doctor Pierce, the doctor who did Matt's reconstruction surgery, came by the room to see Matt. Matt greeted the man as a complete stranger when he walked in the room. Since Matt didn't remember the month that he'd been in the ICU, Matt had not recognized Doctor Pierce.

"Man," Dr. Pierce said, "it's good to hear your voice." Then he explained to Matt who he was, and Matt got teary-eyed and thanked him for what he'd done. During their conversation, the doctor asked for permission to share Matt's story, to which Matt agreed. I'm sure that Matt's miracle story of surviving the tree impalement through the chest made him someone his doctors and nurses would remember for a long, long time.

On Monday, Matt had therapy again and this time they had him climb a set of stairs in the therapy room and he did great! They were amazed at how well he did and said a new recommendation would be to go home and have home health care come to us.

I gripped Matt's hand as the doctor explained how home health care would work. "Are you kidding?" I asked. "Because I can't take a let down from this news."

HOME. It was so close, I could smell it. So, Monday began with preparations for discharge for the next day. I couldn't believe it. Instead of spending Thanksgiving in the hospital or a hotel, we might be home. I didn't want to get my hopes up, but they were doing all the paperwork and consulting to put that plan in place.

"Oh, that I might have my request,
that God would grant what I hope for."

(Job 6:8) New International Version

DAY 44

Tuesday morning, I got up, packed my bags, and had a quick breakfast at the hotel. And for the last time, I checked out at the front desk since today was the day they said Matt was going home. Matt waited anxiously for me, and when I got there, we sat together waiting for word about his official discharge. During the weekend, and even since he'd been in this room, there was truly little communication from the hospital, and Matt was not seen by many people. He was doing fine and didn't need it, so it was time to go home. The physician's assistant who had spoken with us the day before about going home, who also had been on an ICU rotation during Matt's time there, came into the room. I didn't like the look on her face. I knew that what she was about to tell us was not going to be to our liking. I guessed it.

"I'm sorry," she said. "Matt isn't going home just yet." She was just as disappointed as we were. She had wanted to be the one to discharge Matt, but he needed to stay one more night to monitor his breathing overnight. Apparently, and not something we had been made aware of over the past few nights, the nurses had been putting oxygen nose tubes on Matt for this breathing.

Nothing had been said until the process to discharge that day. So, now they needed to keep him one more day and do some tests to make sure he could breathe on his own or if he needed to be sent home with oxygen. I was frustrated, upset, mad, and overcome with disappointment. If he didn't get to go home by Wednesday, the next day was Thanksgiving and the holiday weekend, and I knew nothing would happen during that time.

I asked so many questions that day. I wanted to know exactly what they were going to do in the night and how it would be tracked since someone had failed to do it previously. I wanted to know who was in charge and how all this would change the plans. I tried my best to make sure he went home the next day.

That evening, I stayed until someone came in and let me know the plan. It was an hour past visiting hours and some of the nurses were giving me looks for it.

"You know," one said, though not unkindly, "visiting hours are over."

I said, "Yes, but I'm not leaving until I know exactly what the plan is."

It's funny how sometimes the squeaky wheel really does get the grease. Within a little while, people started showing up and getting things ready for the night. I was able to speak with a respiratory therapist, nurse, and doctor to make sure that everyone knew that this needed to be done because I wanted to go home tomorrow. I found a hotel room and settled myself in for one (I hoped) last night.

The next morning, I woke up feeling positive that today was the day. At the back of my mind, I cautioned myself not to get too excited or hopeful. I would not believe we were going home until I got the car, put Matt in it, and headed west back home. After the let down from the day before, I tried not to anticipate anything and to just go with the flow of the day. I was up as early as I could to get to the hospital to find out the results from the previous evening and if they would allow Matt to go home.

Matt hadn't heard anything yet, but he did say they hadn't put the oxygen on at night. We waited and decided he should order breakfast so that he didn't get hungry. Finally, someone came around and said he'd had trouble breathing but he'd recovered on his own, without support, so he was good to go. Once the doctors finished their rounds and got everything together, Matt would be going home!

Every thirty minutes to an hour, which felt like an eternity, a small development would happen toward going home.

He needed a walker. Ordered and delivered.

Matt needed prescriptions.

We had to pack all his things.

Finally, after several hours, all the papers for discharge were delivered, and all medication prescriptions were filled. This was finally it. We were going home together! No more hotels or driving alone. God performs miracles and, after what we'd gone through, this was a true miracle for Matt to be going home healthy.

"Rejoice in the Lord always. I will say it again: Rejoice!"

(Phil 4:4) New International Version

DAY 1

BACK HOME

After coming home, we needed a few days to get acclimated. The home health people from Carle Hospital in our local area were not coming yet since it was the Thanksgiving weekend. Our kids were there when we got home, and together we got Matt in the house. Ryan, Nicole, and I started getting things set for Matt to be able to take a shower and the bed for whenever he was ready or needed to lay down. Then the next day, Nicole cooked our holiday meal, and we had time with just us to celebrate and be extremely thankful for being together and at home. We took one day at a time and enjoyed family time. I loved seeing Matt back home, in his space, and enjoying the freedom of being with his family.

The next few weeks were busy with initial occupational therapy, physical therapy, and speech and language therapy visits. When each therapist arrived, they would look at Matt and exclaim how impressed they were. Each said that, from reading his chart, they had expected someone who was having difficulty walking and moving around. Matt shocked them when he could open the door. The speech therapist noted that the "patient was better than expected" and did not charge for the visit but still sat and listened to our story. Pure amazement came over all three therapists that worked with Matt for the next three weeks. Other than medical personnel, we had asked for no visitors. With Covid still highly present, we didn't want to risk Matt getting sick.

Thanksgiving the day after Matt was released from the hospital.

Once at home, I decided to wait until January to return to work, but I found out that the two days in December before winter break were workdays with no students so I went back to get my classroom ready and to do report cards. I had missed an entire quarter of school and had a lot to do to catch up and prepare for the return to school.

By the time December rolled around a few days later, we were all settled back home. It's amazing how quickly we were able to return to our routine, surrounded by our pets and back in the home where we'd created so many memories. December, for us, has always been a month for rejoicing. It's a time of year to enjoy family and celebrate the birth of Jesus. Even though we were busy planning holiday get-togethers, just being able to take things slow and at our pace meant a lot. I wanted this Christmas to be special, full of family and laughter.

About a week before Christmas, my dad was in the hospital again. He had so many ailments and, with his age, there was not much more the doctors could do. It was tough hearing he was being sent home and put on hospice. My mom originally wanted to do an open house style of Christmas where only one family at a time would come to the house. But after many rounds of conversations and text messages, it was decided we would all be together that weekend. Matt stayed home since he was still very much at risk of getting sick and there would be so many people in a small space.

My mother's house was a buzz of sadness but joyful memories. My dad had a good day. We got him out of bed and in a wheelchair, and he joined us at the table for lunch. We took many family photos, knowing these might be the last with Dad. Spending time with the family that had just supported me during one of the hardest times in my life, and being together during another ridiculously tough time, was especially important.

By the time the new year rolled around—2022—I had to return to work. It wasn't easy. After missing an entire quarter and being out for two and a half months, so many emotions went through me as I thought about going back. Was it okay to leave Matt alone all day? How would my students be upon my return? Would I worry about Matt? Would I bring home some sickness and give it to my immune-compromised husband?

My whole life, I believed I should have faith that everything unfolds as it should. God does not put one through more than they can handle. To this day, I'm still trying to understand and build on the events of 2021.

I jumped back into school full force, though I remained at a physical distance from my students and asked for air hugs to continue protecting Matt. It was exceedingly difficult for me, as it's my nature to be loving and give hugs to any child that wants one, but a lot of effort went into keeping germs at bay. As soon as I walked in the door at home, I took off all my clothes, washed the bottoms of my shoes, and took a shower before touching my husband. I didn't want to risk any respiratory issues with him in his vulnerable state.

After being back at work one week, I visited my parents' house that weekend in order to see my dad. The next day, Sunday, I felt the need to go back after having been there the whole day before. After returning home, I knew it was time for Dad to go to heaven and, around midnight, my sister called to say he was gone. I couldn't sleep, so I did my lesson plans for school and drove to Mom's to be with her, and my sister and brothers. I then, unfortunately, missed another week of work, to help with arrangements and attend services for Dad.

"Blessed are those who mourn,
for they will be comforted."

(Matt 5:4) New International Version

WHAT MATT REMEMBERS

As January progressed, Matt had a few follow-up appointments with doctors. One day, as I was leaving for work, he mentioned he was going with his dad to the fire and rescue station near the accident site. Matt seemed excited to be able to go to the station, but I felt a little nervous about him returning to the site of his accident. So much trauma was associated with that place that I wasn't sure I'd even be able to drive by without feeling a shudder at what we went through—at what *could* have happened that night.

Unbeknownst to either of us, his dad had called ahead to let them know Matt was coming. They had the guys who helped him that October day there to meet him. They were glad to be able to meet Matt personally since that doesn't happen very often for successful outcomes. While I was eating my lunch and perusing Facebook, I saw the post the station made about Matt's visit. I cried reading through the post, how each of the men there had contributed to saving my husband's life. The amazement never ends thinking of what Matt went through and what the people on the scene thought when they arrived and saw him. Below is Matt's account of what he remembers that day, up until the paramedics put him into a coma. Then his next memory was about thirty-five days later.

The crew and I were working in a remote location in western Indiana near the Illinois border fixing a pipeline. The forecast called for thunderstorms in the area later that day. Throughout the entire day I kept an eye on the radar and the path of the storm. Late afternoon, the sky began to look like rain and the radar showed that it was nearing where we were working. As it began to sprinkle, we loaded up our tools and returned to our vehicles. The rain got harder, so we called it a day. The crew headed south while I headed west toward home. As I was driving toward the main road, the wind grew stronger, and I noticed some sticks breaking and falling. Then, all of the sudden, there was a big commotion—the world around me shook and I registered that my vehicle had been hit by something *big*. After it all stopped, I found my car had been pushed off the road and I was stuck in the ditch. I noticed my windshield was shattered. Then, in the upper driver side corner of the windshield, I noticed a tree limb. My eyes followed the limb to my chest. Instinct led my hands to the limb, and I tried to pull it out, but it would not budge. It was then that I realized I was hurt badly, and I needed help. Somehow, I backed the car up and pulled it forward, working my car out of the ditch and back onto the road. I then began driving. I knew that not many cars would be on this road, and I needed to get to a main road to get help. My breathing felt difficult, though at the time I'm not sure I registered any pain.

As I drove, I dialed the one person that was on my mind. My wife. After a few rings, I hung up as she didn't answer, and I dialed 911. I didn't know exactly where I was but gave them a general location while telling them that I had a tree limb in my chest. I peered through the cracks in my windshield and into the rain, and thought I saw someone, but they didn't stop. It may have been my mind playing tricks on me, but I vowed that if I drove past someone else, I was not going to let them pass. I drove a little further while talking to 911 and saw a blue van coming my way. I maneuvered my car to the middle of the road so that the driver had to stop. I told the 911 dispatcher that I'd stopped someone in the road, and they were approaching my vehicle. I will never forget the man's face when he got out of his van—first angry and then wide-eyed as he took me in, comprehending why I'd stopped him. Though I couldn't see myself, I could only imagine what a horrible vision I was. The man helped 911, speaking with the dispatcher when I couldn't, and provided them with a more exact location. He grabbed a rag and tried staunching some of my bleeding. He then had me talk to 911 to keep me awake.

"Are you married?" the man asked. My eyes felt heavy.

"Yes," I remember saying. "Can you call my wife?"

I don't remember if we spoke after that, but I do remember glimpses of light through the windshield and knew that help was arriving. I remember thinking to myself if I can get this limb out, then I can go home. Faces appeared in the window and kept me talking. I remember a man with a mustache, though I don't know what his job was. The responders cut into my car to extricate me and I had a moment where I felt sad, knowing the car was unsalvageable.

Then, a kind woman sat in the seat next to me and I told her I was having a hard time breathing. She said "We're working on that." So much was going on, and then I remember feeling calm and being lifted out of my seat.

Matt was extricated from his car.

The next thing I remember was nearly thirty days later. The entirety of my hospital stay feels like something out of a dream. I feel like I saw doctors and nurses. I feel like my wife held my hand. But none of it was sure in my mind until it was confirmed by others who were there. Other dreams, I found out, truly were just that—my mind playing tricks on me. One of my first truly lucid memories—around day 35 of my stay in the ICU—was that I was able to use my phone to look up who was in the world series. It was then I truly grasped that I'd been out for several weeks.

Seeing such a time marker for myself, rather than hearing about it, really made me realize how long I hadn't been present in daily life. Being unaware of the amount of time that had actually passed and how much I'd missed was—and still is—hard for me to comprehend.

*"And we know that in all things God
works for the good of those who love him,
who have been called according to his purpose."*

(Rom 8:28) New International Version

EPILOGUE

By the end of January, Matt was progressing nicely and was thinking about returning to work in February. He had been walking and exercising and had built up the strength to return. Each day, Matt would walk laps in our shed, increasing the number each day. What a blessing it was for both of us to see him able to function like normal after such an ordeal.

Matt wanted to meet the surgeon who had performed the surgery to remove the tree limb, so he called and made an appointment with the doctor. I was overly nervous about meeting him and wondered what he might think about us coming. The anticipation was killing me as we sat in a waiting area for Matt's name to be called. After what seemed like an eternity, Matt was called back to a room. After a few more minutes of waiting, the doctor came in and shook Matt's hand, in awe of how well he looked. He looked at Matt's scars, talked about the whole ordeal and shared pictures that had been taken the evening of the accident. The doctor said this was a first. He had to call maintenance after Matt arrived at the ER to request a Sawzall to cut down the limb in order to get Matt into the operating room. Matt was so glad to talk to him and hear his thoughts. The visit ended with a photo of the two of them together.

Dr. Lynch the doctor that removed the tree limb.

Matt returned to work on February 10, 2022, just shy of four months from the day of the accident. It was a day filled with moments to cherish. The previous months had been tough, but he was well and ready to share his story.

Later in February, while just enjoying a normal day of work, Matt's phone rang from a number he didn't recognize. He answered and the caller launched into rapid-fire sentences, talking super-fast and extremely excited. The lady on the phone talked about how she didn't know he had visited their office, she was disappointed she hadn't been there to see him, and that she wanted to plan a reunion at the hospital. Matt had to slow her down and ask who she was. It was the chief medical officer, Doctor Lawson, who had done the first surgery to remove the tree limb from Matt's chest that fateful day in October.

Due to the doctor's excitement and her being a fast talker, all Matt understood from the phone call was that she wanted to set up a time for him to meet people from the day of the accident. Matt tried to pay attention to what she was saying and agreed to the meeting and waited for the next phone call to finalize the reunion plans.

After some planning, the reunion was set for March, during my spring break. I really was glad this had come up at the right time, so I didn't have to take off work. Matt and I made plans to go to the hospital. The agenda was not completely clear for me. All communication had been through Matt, and I based my expectations upon what he told me. The morning of the reunion came, and I was a little nervous to say the least.

Since my nerves were getting the best of me, I only ate half a bagel for breakfast before our 8:00 a.m. meeting with the Chief Medical Officer. However, it was an oddly serene feeling, walking into the hospital for the first time since October—like greeting an old, comfortable friend. I scanned the familiar lobby, remembering that night of the accident and pointing out places to Matt. Then I saw the doctor and two others walking our way. We said our greetings and were introduced to the chief nursing officer and the CEO of the hospital. The group led us into a staff area and we were taken to the surgery area that was not open yet for the day. As we were talking, more people arrived. Most had been told to come for a meeting, but we *were* the meeting.

It was interesting to hear the medical staff talk about where they were and what they had been doing when the Level 1 trauma call was put out. Realizing that these people gave up family time to answer the call to return to work to help a trauma patient puts into perspective what life in the medical field is like. They were asked to drop what they are doing—giving their child a bath, having a delicious, relaxing dinner with a spouse—to respond to my husband's case. Had they not, Matt wouldn't have been standing here with me, either.

There were no words to describe the thankfulness we have for people like this. After meeting staff in the operating area, we went to a meeting with all the nurses and medical staff who were preparing for the day of surgeries. We were introduced and the room took on a whole new meaning. They were just as surprised to see us as we were to see them. Matt spoke for a minute, thanking them for what they do. I don't know how he spoke; I was choked up just standing there listening and meeting these people. Right before we left, he asked if anyone in the room was there that night. A few hands in the back went up and he just looked at them and said thanks.

Next up was a walk to the emergency room. We walked through the doors and were told we would go into a conference room while the team gathered to meet us. But, as we walked through the doors, a guy standing at the nurse's station spotted us and said, "Hey! Is that the tree guy?"

Our surprise had been blown. The paramedic from that day had been called to the ER that morning for a briefing, along with the lead nurse and other staff who had been on duty on October 11. We then went into a trauma bay and spent the next thirty minutes talking, listening to their thoughts, crying together, embracing each other—these men and women who saved my husband's life.

⌒

March 30, 2022, ended up being a day of significant importance for Matt and me. The Indianapolis hospital called and wanted Matt's story. We eagerly agreed. Over the phone, the representative from the marketing department explained they wanted to make a big publicity announcement at the Indy 500, the weekend of May 29. Matt had been selected, from their numerous patients of the previous year, to be the Green Flag Delivery Honoree, along with two other people. We would fly in a helicopter to the speedway the morning of the race. This was huge for us as, even though we live fairly close, we had never been to the Indianapolis 500.

Matt asked about going the night before and the hospital representative agreed to check on that for us. Within the next few days, documents were emailed for us to sign. As in the days in the hospital, we had to sign waivers and releases. But this opportunity was a no-brainer and sign away we did. We were told to keep it private until it was closer to race day so they could get it set up.

That same day, the marketing department from the hospital that removed the tree limb contacted us about doing a story for a weekly news blast. It was a very emotional, big day with a lot going on while we still tried to work without being able to tell anyone. That evening at home, we researched delivering the green flag to find out more about what it involves.

From that day on March 30th to race day on May 29th, our lives were remarkably busy, filled with phone calls to arrange times to meet with marketing for the two different hospitals to finish our story and prepare for news and race day. Throughout the month of April, Matt talked with a representative from the Indianapolis hospital. We had many questions and tried to schedule a reunion with the staff from the Surgical Trauma ICU. We still weren't allowed to tell our friends and family about all the good things happening in May with the Race weekend.

However, on April 24th, the first airing of news shared about Matt's accident. Union Health marketing had been working with us and others involved to air two-minute segments on the local TV station. The first of four parts aired on April 24th, sharing the beginning of our story. Over the next four weeks, a two-minute segment aired with interviews with medical staff about Matt's impalement.

After watching the segment myself, I then shared it on my Facebook page. Matt and I felt it was particularly important to share with others how God had worked in our lives, so I shared it and when I checked, it had a total of seven shares. On each share were comments, not only from people we knew but complete strangers. The hardest part of that first segment was the 911 call Matt made. Listening to this call for the first time sent chills down my spine as I heard him asking for help. The comments after people watched spoke to how much his story can mean to others.

Matt, you are a miracle!

God was surely watching over him that day!

God is good all the time.

Unbelievable simply unbelievable.

Chills just listening . . . no doubt God was in control.

I cannot even imagine how he continued to drive for help without God watching out for him... there is no other explanation. God was with him, making sure Matt was going to live. Truly another chance at life, as it was not yet his time. God has greater plans for him here on earth.

Amazing.

Each week, we would anticipate the airing of the next segment and share it with everyone on Facebook. We also shared the final plans for the IU Health reunion and TV interview to announce IU Health's selection of Matt, myself, and one of his nurses as the ones to deliver the green flag to the Indianapolis 500 on race day. We had already made some plans for race day, and had gotten tickets for our kids to join us at the race. We might not be in the same section but having them there for this momentous moment was important.

May 15, Matt and I headed to Indianapolis for an overnight stay before the meeting. On our way we made a stop at the ambulance company to reunite with the team that first worked with Matt at the scene. After several hours of talking and Matt hearing their versions of that day and the outcome, we took a picture and then headed on over to Indy. It was very strange to go back and stay at one of the hotels I had stayed at for almost two weeks while Matt was in the hospital. When checking in, I was reminded why I liked this hotel. The staff were so professional and truly took care of their guests.

Matt and I went out for a nice dinner that night and got a good night's rest before our big day at the downtown heliport the next day. We woke up, got ready, and drove downtown. We parked and sat and waited trying to decide when we could head inside since we were a bit early. It was hard to sit still in the car and wait so, when it was close to time, we headed up to the door and buzzed to be let in. We were escorted upstairs. We met with the representatives from marketing and were briefed on what would take place. We met the newscaster from the TV station doing the interview.

After about fifteen minutes, all participants had arrived, and we knew we were being filmed, and the reunion was under way.

We had no idea who had been asked to come and meet us but when I saw the familiar faces of Beth and Kelly, who were incredibly special to me during the days in the hospital, I was very emotional. As Doctor Pierce, Beth, Kelly and the chaplain walked across the helipad, it was hard to stay put. As soon as the group reached Matt and I, Beth, who was unable to contain herself any more, ran up and gave me the biggest, longest hug.

We talked, shared, and Matt told the doctor he had a bunch of questions. Once we each got to talk, we then had to complete all our interviews, not only with the television station but with the hospital media team. Two different videos were made for broadcast at separate times.

The surgeon that reconstructed Matt's Chest.

After a few hours, we then said we wanted to go back to the hospital to meet with the other nurses who played a part in helping Matt recover. We made the short drive and met the chaplain, Beth, and Kelly in the lobby, and we made our way up to the surgical trauma critical care unit. Walking into the unit, we met with Renee, Alex, Elanor, and a few others. They even called Jamie on her day off and she came over to the hospital too. It was so good to see them, and Matt enjoyed meeting them. He still didn't remember all that happened, but he was finally putting faces to the names of the nurses I talked about.

Then we said our goodbyes and I showed Matt some of the places I had frequented during those long days. There was a courtyard that was nice to sit in for fresh air. We got some lunch and headed home so we could watch the live stream of the TV station news cast. We were finally able to share with everyone our good news about being honored on race day.

Neither Matt nor I had ever been to the Indy 500. We knew that Indianapolis takes on a whole new face that weekend, with so many coming to town for the race. We had been given a hotel reservation for the night before the race since we had to be there so early. The night before race day, Matt and I spent some time reflecting and anticipating the next day. We also decided to go to see the new *Top Gun* movie, since the lead in the film would be the actor we would hand the flag to on race day. It seemed appropriate as the first *Top Gun* movie was one of our favorites. I did not get much sleep that night. My alarm went off early so I could get up and be ready for the day ahead.

The next day, upon arriving at the heliport, we were met with a bustle of activity. Tourist helicopters were taking people to the race. Kelly was there with her daughter and parents. We anxiously awaited the signal to go out and take pictures at the helicopter. Then it was time to get in and wait for takeoff. After some confusion about where people were allowed to sit and also the approval for take-off, we were ready to fly. It was a short ride, but we took in every minute. As we approached the speedway, I could see the people in the stands. All these small dots down below us just doing their own thing. Did they realize we were flying all the way in? Did they know what the helicopter was for?

As we approached the speedway, we made our way along the track between the two tall seating areas where the race starts. We landed and got out of the helicopter to make our way to a waiting car. Matt and I got in the lead car and Kelly got in the second car. While Matt was holding the green flag, we slowly started moving and began our way around the track.

Indy 500 Helicopter which is the same helicopter that flew me from Terre Haute to Indianapolis on the evening of the accident.

When we reached the starting line, we got out of the car and were trying to figure out where to go. We had been told we would go on stage and hand the flag to Miles Teller, the *Top Gun* actor. However, the delay taking off from the helipad made us late for that part and the five hundred staff had moved on since they were on a tight schedule. We contacted someone to ask questions but stayed inside the track as long as we could watch all the drivers, cars, and people. They were starting to close off the area to spectators and so we waited until we knew for sure what to do before leaving. The race representative was sorry we had missed meeting Miles Teller, but took the green flag to him, had him sign it, and then they said we could keep it.

The rest of the day went smoothly. We went to the suite and got food to eat. Then we made our way to the rooftop for the start of the race. There were two different eating times in the suite and so we ate again. We were certainly full and content.

Once the race was over, we met up with the kids, said our goodbyes to everyone, and walked out of the speedway to head home. We were tired, but had a memorable day and were glad to get in our car and head toward home.

Having the opportunity to attend the race and deliver the green flag was an amazing experience. Getting to share the story and reunite with the nurses and doctors made for a fantastic way to end our journey of this impalement trauma. During this traumatic time in our lives, leaning on our faith in God helped us to keep moving forward. Having a prayer community available through our friends from across the United States helped to build our strength in trusting that God can heal and answer prayers big and small. If you ever find yourself in a similar situation, seek guidance and prayer from other Christians and churches in your community. Listen to verses or songs to uplift your thoughts of hope. Without God, this could have been a very dark, extremely sorrowful time in our lives. Instead, with God we found strength.

"For from him and through him and for him are all things. To him be the glory forever! Amen."

(Rom 11:36) New International Version

ACKNOWLEDGEMENTS

T hank you to Marilyn Coartney who stood by me and didn't let me give up. She spent an entire day with me going page by page, offering suggestions for the development of the book. Thank you to Josh Powell for reading the manuscript and offering helpful suggestions. Special thanks to my editor Tarah Threadgill for great insights for the development of the book.

I appreciate the guidance and wisdom provided by Katya Fishman of Endeavorink, for coaching us through the book process.

Lastly, we want to give God the glory for His Grace and Blessings. Through Him we can share this story of how God worked in our lives.

REFLECTIONS AND HIGHLIGHTS

Matt and I believe our experiences in 2021 hold valuable lessons that we are eager to share with others. We are open to sharing about our experience and our faith and how God helps us get through situations in our lives, and we passionately believe God has a unique purpose for each person on this earth. We constantly reflect on what we learned during this traumatic time, seeking ways to use our story to uplift and inspire others, acknowledging that life is a meaningful journey even when our paths are not always clear.

Thank you for reading our book. We would love to hear from you. Please feel free to email us at: Matt and Jill Cheatham rainydaymiracle@gmail.com

For more information and videos about Matt's accident and journey please feel free to scan this QR code to reach our author's Facebook page.

www.ingramcontent.com/pod-product-compliance
Lightning Source LLC
Chambersburg PA
CBHW071754120626
46550CB00002B/784